C000192655

TRADED OPTIONS - A PRIVATE INVESTOR'S GUIDE

This publication has been produced by B T Batsford and LIFFE Administration and Management (LIFFE), Whilst all reasonable care has been taken to ensure details are true and not misleading at the time of publication, no liability is accepted by LIFFE, nor their servants or agents, for the use of information contained herein in any circumstances connected with actual trading or otherwise. Neither B T Batsford, LIFFE nor their servants or agents, are responsible for any errors or omissions within this book. It is published for information purposes only and shall not constitute investment advice. All descriptions, examples and calculations contained in this book are for guidance purposes only and should not be treated as definitive. LIFFE reserves the right to alter any of its rules or contract specifications, and such an event may affect the validity of the information contained in this book. The FTSE 100 Index is compiled by the London Stock Exchange. The FTSE 100 is a member of the FTSE Actuaries Share Indices which are calculated in accordance with a standard set of rules established by the Financial Times Limited and The London Stock Exchange in conjunction with the Institute of Actuaries and the Faculty of Actuaries. 'FTSE' and 'Footsie' are joint trade marks and service marks of the London Stock Exchange and the Financial Times Limited, © The International Stock Exchange of the United Kingdom and Republic of Ireland Limited 1994. All rights reserved.

TRADED OPTIONS - A PRIVATE INVESTOR'S GUIDE

How to invest more profitably

Peter Temple

B. T. BATSFORD LTD · LONDON

Batsford Business Online: www.batsford.com

First published 1995
This edition 1998

© London International Financial
Futures and Options Exchange (LIFFE)

All rights reserved. No part of this publication may be reproduced,
sorted in a removal system,or transmitted in any form or by any means,
electronic, mechanical, photocopying, recording or otherwise without
the prior permission of the publisher.

The right of Peter Temple to be identified as the author of this work
has been asserted by him in accordance with the Copyright, Designs
and Patents Act 1988.

A CIP catalogue record for this book is available from The British
Library.

ISBN 0 7134 8445 4

Published by:
B T Batsford Ltd,
583 Fulham Road,
London SW6 5BY
and sponsored by
London International Financial
Futures and Options Exchange

Printed by
Redwood Books
Trowbridge
Wiltshire

CONTENTS

FOREWORD

As I wrote in the Foreword to the first edition of this book three years ago, a low level of understanding has surely been a major factor in the relatively slow growth of interest taken by private clients in the UK equity and index options market. Although there are some signs this is changing, I am nonetheless delighted again to write a brief introduction to this book, sponsored by LIFFE, which sets out to improve the overall level of awareness of the options market among private investors.

LIFFE is undeniably the largest financial futures and options exchange in Europe and, on many trading days, its volume rivals the largest American exchanges. It offers the widest range of products available at any exchange in the world. The market for derivative products, such as financial futures and options, in the UK is a thriving one. Professional trading of LIFFE's interest rate products has, with the exception of a brief pause in 1995, broken records every year since the market was formed in 1982. Last year, which saw the 15th anniversary of the market's inception, was again a record year.

However, despite the fact that equity options have been traded in London for 20 years, the 'retail' market is only now beginning to realise its potential. Equity and index options have had a consistent degree of commitment from the exchange since it became responsible for the market in 1992. This approach is beginning to produce positive results and the private client market is one in which we fully expect to see continuing and substantial growth in the future.

But there is still a long way to go. One only has to look to Europe and the US to find proof that private investors are able to make valuable and extensive use of these products. While private client trading in equity and index options accounts for less than 20% of the market in the UK, private clients in Holland account for nearly 70% of a volume figure almost four times that seen in the UK. And all this in a country whose population is a quarter that of the UK.

As with so many things, though, a little knowledge can be a dangerous thing and it is vitally important that people take time to understand options, as they should any other financial instrument, before committing money to dealing in them.

Virtually all of the work undertaken by LIFFE to develop any of its products is of an educational nature. This is especially true in respect of the private client market for equity and index options, where the Exchange offers a wide range of printed material and courses, an introductory video, and access to a range of information via its web site.

I believe that this book has been and will continue to be a very useful component of the wide range of information on the subject and will be of great use to those investors who are new to options as well as those who, having identified the potential benefits, require some further guidance to enable their participation in the market. The new edition both updates earlier material to allow for recent and prospective new developments in the market, and contains an entirely new chapter devoted to the increasing range of resources available for option investors on the world wide web, a development in which LIFFE has been pleased to play its part.

As before, it is also my hope that this book will continue to dispel some of the myths that surround options - myths which, like so many others, are often based on hearsay rather than understanding, and which frequently prevent people making valuable discoveries for themselves.

Daniel Hodson
Chief Executive
LIFFE
Cannon Bridge
London EC4R 3XX

May 1998

ABOUT LIFFE

Background

In March 1992, the London International Financial Futures Exchange merged with the London Traded Options Market to create the London International Financial Futures and Options Exchange - LIFFE for short. LIFFE's membership currently comprises around 200 firms, including some of the largest UK and international banks and securities houses. As a Recognised Investment Exchange (RIE) under the 1986 Financial Services Act, LIFFE regulates the operation of the market itself, in compliance with the requirements of the Act.

The Exchange, located at Cannon Bridge in the City of London, fulfils a vital role as a market place where users such as financial institutions, corporate treasury departments and commercial investors, as well as private individuals, can trade and manage financial risk. LIFFE's trading floor was specifically designed for derivatives trading and remains arguably the most sophisticated trading environment currently available in the world.

Thanks to London's geographical position in the European time zone, LIFFE's trading hours extend from late in the Asian trading day to the first few hours of the US markets, and its user profile and membership is correspondingly international.

When it was formed in 1982, the Exchange initially offered a limited number of interest rate products, but has since developed liquid and transparent markets in many bond, money market, stock index and equity market products. Indeed, LIFFE now provides the most comprehensive range of financial futures and options products traded on any exchange in the world. The 1996 merger with the London Commodity Exchange also brought into the LIFFE fold trading in futures and options on a variety of agricultural commodities.

LIFFE Equity Products

Options, in one form or another, have been traded since the Middle Ages, but it was only relatively recently that London was able to offer investors exchange-traded equity options. Trading first started in April 1978, when the London Stock

Exchange listed 'call' options (which confer the right to buy) on the shares of 10 leading companies. 'Put' options (the corresponding right to sell) were introduced three years later. Since those early days, investor demand has prompted the market to expand, and LIFFE now offers put and call options on the shares of more than 70 leading UK companies, as well as futures and options on the FTSE 100 index, and futures on the FTSE 250 index. During the past year, the average value of underlying turnover in LIFFE's equity products has comfortably exceeded £3bn per day.

Many new initiatives are currently in the process of development. November 1998, for example, will see the transfer of equity options trading to an electronic environment. In addition, new products are constantly being researched and LIFFE remains actively involved in the education of traders, institutional investors, and private individuals alike.

The Exchange recognises the importance of the 'retail' investor market and is committed to developing private client option business in the UK through awareness raising and education, a process which also encompasses those brokers who deal for private investors. The market development team at LIFFE continues to address the needs of an expanding market by providing a wide range of educational material and seminars throughout the year and by constantly reviewing the needs of those wishing to incorporate equity and index options into their investment portfolios.

For further information, please contact:

> LIFFE
> Cannon Bridge
> London EC4R 3XX.
>
> Tel: 0171 623 0444
> Fax: 0171 379 2382

AUTHOR'S ACKNOWLEDGEMENTS

Owing to an oversight, no acknowledgements were published in the first edition. The following thanks, therefore, relate to both editions of the book.

As can probably be deduced, LIFFE has been of tremendous help to me in both writing the original version and revising and adding to the text for the second edition. Thanks go in particular to Tony Hawes at LIFFE, for his unstinting help with the first edition, and to Nick Bramley and Michelle Townsend for their help with the second.

Design staff at LIFFE contributed many of the graphs for the first edition from my rough sketches and have been responsible for the cover design for both editions. A debt of thanks is also due to the publications department and press office at the exchange for a steady flow of material. An interview with Fiona King helped flesh out details of LIFFE's web presence.

Many investors have found intermediate level courses taught by Jim Bittman, of the Options Institute, of help, and I was no exception. The section on 'covered writing' flowed directly from one of his lectures and he has my thanks for that.

Away from the exchange, the debts are many and various. Tony Drury originally commissioned the book and saw the first edition through to publication. John Winters at B T Batsford picked up the mantle on behalf of the new publisher. Thanks are also due to Bill Newton, Trevor Neil, Andy Webb, David Charters, Bruce Waugh, Neil Osborne, David Linton and Jeremy duPlessis for completing various parts of my education on the subjects of either options, software, or technical analysis. Steve Vale, at FTSE International, helped explain the intricacies of the FTSE 100 Index. John Ingram, at Winstock, got me up and running with The Analyst software for the chart illustrations for the second edition; Synergy's Mitchell Brooks was of similar help for the first edition. Philip Ryland, deputy editor of the *Investors Chronicle*, has been a keen supporter of the book. Needless to say, any deficiencies that remain are entirely my own doing.

Lastly, a big thank you to my wife, Lynn, and to Claire and David Temple for their forbearance and encouragement during the preparation of both editions.

HOW TO READ THIS BOOK

The terminology and trading procedures of equity and index options can, at first, seem complicated. Therefore each chapter starts with a table of key words and definitions ('Key Terminology'). You will find it helpful to spend a few minutes familiarising yourself with these before starting the step-by-step approach on which this book is structured. As the chapters develop we introduce a number of examples which allow you the opportunity to test your progress. Each example is accompanied by a simple chart showing the expected pattern of profits or losses from the option or option strategy. For simplicity the chart shows the position of a single option. Worked examples may involve the use of multiple numbers of option contracts. This does not affect the profit/loss profile displayed in the chart. Never hesitate to refer back to an earlier chapter if any aspect of the subject remains unclear.

ONE

AN INTRODUCTION TO
EQUITY AND INDEX OPTIONS

This book is about equity and index options (usually known as traded options) and how to invest in them profitably. Investing in options is quite different from investing in shares. Different rules need to be followed, and a disciplined approach must be adopted.

The subject matter of options can be complex, and the day-to-day terminology of the options market needs to be understood thoroughly before any dealing is done. A table of key words and definitions ('Key Terminology') is therefore given in each chapter for easy reference. Please see page 16 for the table covering this chapter.

Above all, investors should remember that options are inherently more volatile than ordinary shares, and there can therefore be more risk involved in investing in them - and, of course, higher returns as well. **The close monitoring of options trades may be necessary.**

Some investors view options solely as speculative vehicles. This is not correct. Though options can be used as a speculative medium, this is not their only application. They can also be used in a variety of ways as part of longer term investment strategies. Above all they are a flexible tool for the management of risk and reward.

Because options terminology is complex, its detail will be explained gradually through the book. Different options concepts will be introduced in stages so that the reader can become familiar with one step before moving on to the next.

This chapter covers what options are, how options markets have developed, basic options concepts and different types of options, the advantages to the private investor of trading in options and a summary of the risks and rewards.

Subsequent chapters look in detail at call options, put options and index options, and the basic strategies related to them. We also examine how to choose a stockbroking firm through which to trade options, more complex option investment strategies, and how charts and computer valuation techniques can be used to facilitate these decisions.

KEY TERMINOLOGY

Call Option - a contract which confers on the holder the right, but not the obligation, to buy a fixed quantity of underlying shares at a specific price for a limited period of time.

Put Option - a contract which confers on the holder the right, but not the obligation, to sell a fixed quantity of underlying shares at a specific price for a limited period of time.

Exercise (or Strike) Price - the price at which the holder of the option buys (call) or sells (put) the underlying shares if he chooses to exercise his right.

Expiry Date - the 'time limit' on the right conferred by the option contract.

Option Premium - the 'price' of the option, paid by the buyer.

Option Series - a specific option defined by its underlying stock, exercise price, expiry date and type. The 'BTR August 360 call' is an example of an option series.

Option Writer - the initial 'seller' of the option. He must undertake the obligation of fulfiling the terms of the option contract should the holder choose to exercise it. He has an obligation, but no rights.

Options and How They Work
It is important at the outset to understand exactly what options are and the nature of their relationship to ordinary shares.

An option takes the form of a contract that gives the holder the right, but not the obligation, to buy or sell a fixed number of shares (normally 1,000 per contract) at a fixed price, on or before a given date. The right conferred by an option can be exercised, but it need not be if it is not in the investor's interest to do so. This is because the holder has rights, but no obligations.

An option can be (and has been) granted over many forms of assets: a house; a car; any form of commodity; and most types of financial assets. In the minds of most investors, however, options relate to ordinary shares. Equity options are options that can be bought and sold in the equity options market. This market is

16

part of the London International Financial Futures and Options Exchange (LIFFE).

How Equity Options Work

Imagine that ICI shares are trading at 750p and you have acquired in the market an option to buy shares in ICI at that price. Because the writer (ie. the seller) of the option is taking a risk in giving you the option, it has a cost. That cost is, say, 25p.

Now imagine the price of ICI shares suddenly goes up by 100p. The option will be worth more. Instead of the underlying share price being roughly the same as that granted by the option - 750p - it is 100p higher. The option could be exercised and the holder make an instant profit by selling in the market - at 850p - the shares being acquired at 750p via the option.

What in fact happens is that the price of the option reflects the change in the underlying share price. Instead of being able to buy the option for 25p, its price might now be around 125p - to reflect the 100p rise in the price of the underlying shares.

One advantage of options is that a given percentage change in the price of the shares can be magnified in the price of the options. In the example of ICI, the price of the shares rose from 750p to 850p, or 13%. The price of the option rose from 25p to around 125p, a gain of some 400%. Although this process can work in reverse if the price of the underlying share falls, the buyer of the option has a strict limit on the loss that will be incurred. **The buyer cannot lose more than the original cost of the option.**

In addition, the outlay involved in buying the option as opposed to the equivalent number of shares is much smaller. Buying 1,000 ICI shares would have cost £7,500. Buying the equivalent one ICI option in the example given would cost £250.

One use of equity options is therefore as a low-cost way of taking advantage of expected movements in individual shares and the stockmarket as a whole.

There are **two** types of option:

■ A **CALL** option is an option to **BUY** shares.

■ A **PUT** option is an option to **SELL** shares.

■ **CALL** options generally **RISE** in price if the underlying shares **RISE.**

■ **PUT** options generally **RISE** in price if the underlying shares **FALL.**

The ease with which options can be bought and sold means that the investor need not hold them just with a view to eventually exercising them, but can instead simply sell in the market if the price moves in the anticipated direction.

An advantage of using options is that dealing costs are confined to those relating to the option contract, and the investor does not necessarily have to find the capital (or the underlying stock) to purchase stock from (or sell to) the person on the other side of the contract.

Take the example of a company whose share price stands at 500p with at-the-money call options priced at 35p. Buying 3000 shares at a cost of £15,000 would attract brokerage commission at say 1.25% from a normal full service broker equating to £187.50, whereas the cost of gaining exposure to the equivalent number of shares through a purchase of three call option contracts would be around £31 - typical minimum commission of £25 plus £2 settlement levy per contract.

In addition, not all shares possess the correct combination of characteristics that will make them suitable in option stocks, so natural selection limits the list to a manageable number. The options market at LIFFE exists to provide a focus of liquidity for trading in options.

Traditional Options

Equity options as traded on LIFFE are not, however, the whole story. There is, for example, a crucial difference between tradeable equity and index options (sometimes known simply as 'traded options') and other types of options on ordinary shares. These latter products are known as 'traditional options'.

The key distinction between traded or equity options and traditional options is that equity options can be freely bought and sold on LIFFE. Traditional options are not tradeable and must therefore simply be bought and held.

This does not mean they are without value. Traditional options are generally available on different shares to those at LIFFE. The normal assumption made when purchasing a traditional option, however, is that it will be held and exercised at the appropriate time. If at that time it proves to be valueless, it will be allowed to lapse and the investment in it written off.

Traditional options lack the flexibility possessed by equity options. They, too have a limited life, extending only to three months. Equity and index options are available over both longer and shorter periods.

Traditional options have another disadvantage. Both the buyer and the seller of a traditional option are locked into an inflexible arrangement for the life of the option - irrespective of what happens to the underlying share price or to either party's financial circumstances.

They remain, in effect, partners throughout the life of the option. The contract is a bilateral one and cannot be passed on by either of them to a third party. However, they can be valued and analysed in the same way as equity options.

How Options Markets Developed

Options have existed for a long time. The concept and theory behind options probably dates back to the development of the law of contract in mediaeval times. For many centuries since that time options have been used in a simple way to oil the wheels of trade in agricultural produce, imports, and manufactured products. Options of one form or another have been granted, and bought and sold, since the origins of the Stock Exchange in the City of London's coffee houses in the 17th century.

Over the years, however, options at various times had a rather unsavoury reputation. They were, for instance, part and parcel of the tulip bulb boom and subsequent bust in 17th century Holland. They played a role during the 1920s on Wall Street and were held to be one of the reasons behind the 1929 crash. And after the 1987 stockmarket crash voices were also raised blaming futures and options for the debacle. Proponents of the options market feel these accusations are unfair.

For much of this time, however, options contracts were traded only informally on a bilateral basis between individuals and organisations. This informal market still exists today. Now known as the 'over-the-counter' market in options, such bilateral deals represent a large and growing component of the overall market for what are collectively known as 'derivatives'.

Derivatives, such as options and financial futures, are financial instruments whose price movements are derived from the price movement of an underlying security or asset.

The growth of the 'over-the-counter' derivatives market has become a source of concern for governments and market participants alike, chiefly because of its largely unregulated nature.

The notion of creating standardised options that could be traded through an exchange was devised in Chicago and first introduced in 1973, when the Chicago Board Options Exchange - the CBOE - was established. The key adaptations to the traditional options market introduced alongside the creation of the CBOE were: first, the standardisation of the exercise price and expiry date of the contract; and second, the development of interchangeability of options contracts. This cut the link tying the buyer and seller of the traditional option together, thus giving back flexibility to both parties to the transaction.

Another factor encouraging the development of options that could be traded through an exchange was the fact that work by American academics at the time had come up with a way of accurately valuing them - the so-called Black-Scholes model, whose three authors were recently awarded the Nobel Prize for Economics.

The trading of options in a recognised exchange in London began in April 1978 with the creation of the London Traded Options Market (LTOM) under the aegis of the London Stock Exchange. Initially, call options (that is, those conferring the right to buy a share at a specific exercise, or 'strike', price) were listed on the shares of ten leading companies. Put options (those conferring the right to sell) on the same shares came three years later.

19

Over the course of the 1980s, demand for options was such that the number of shares covered by the traded options market gradually expanded to the point where put and call options on over 70 leading shares are now offered, each with a variety of strike prices and expiry dates.

As individual company fortunes have ebbed and flowed over the course of this seventeen year period, so the composition of the list has changed. Of the original shares with options listed in 1978, seven remain. These are BP, Commercial Union, GEC, ICI, Land Securities, Marks & Spencer, and Shell.

As part of the process of refining and updating the market to reflect demand from LIFFE's own membership and investor interest, the roster of options companies changes from time to time. Options on some shares have been removed because of takeovers (Eastern Electricity) and a handful have disappeared because of bankruptcy(Polly Peck and Ferranti). Several new options stocks have emerged through demergers (Centrica, Imperial Tobacco), or because of large scale flotations and demutualisations (Halifax, Alliance & Leicester).

Of over 70 companies for which equity options are currently available, all but a small minority are FTSE 100 constituents. Some of these companies may have started out as FTSE 100 index constituents but have subsequently been removed from the index because they failed to meet the necessary test for inclusion, because of a relative decline in their stockmarket value. Traded options are also available on the FTSE 100 index itself.

The exodus of share dealing from the stockmarket floor after 'Big Bang' in 1986 left the LTOM dealers clustered in a corner of a much larger trading area. It also removed the original rationale for being there - proximity to dealings in the underlying shares on which the equity options contracts were based.

The Development of LIFFE
While LIFFE's turnover in financial futures was growing in leaps and bounds through the 1980s and beyond, LTOM's began to languish. One reason was the October 1987 stockmarket crash. Not only did this result in much lower share prices for a time, but it also led to a sharp contraction in the volume of shares being traded.

More serious was the small but well-publicised number of individuals who had lost spectacular sums as a result of ill-judged trading in the options market. The result was a reduction in options turnover.

The upshot of all this was a merger between LIFFE and LTOM, perhaps more accurately described as LIFFE's absorption of the traded options market. This took place on 23rd March 1992 and more or less coincided with the move of the futures exchange from the Royal Exchange to the purpose-built trading floor at Cannon Bridge, a large office block in the City.

Since the merger with LTOM, LIFFE has mounted a number of initiatives to revive interest in equity options. These have included obvious measures like modifying the range of equity options offered. But there have also been other, less well-publicised, developments. One of these has been the establishment of a programme of education and training for existing and potential users of the market, including private investors.

Equity products, as defined by LIFFE, include not only individual equity options, but also index futures and options. Volumes of all categories of equity product have been rising in recent years, but the gains have been most dramatic in the case of index futures and options.

Working in LIFFE's favour in this regard have been changes in the UK tax and regulatory environments which allow UK-based institutional investors to make more use of the futures and options market than hitherto. While the rules still limit 'speculation' in options by fund managers, these products can now be used, in conjunction with related transactions in the underlying shares, to hedge or change the make-up of assets in a particular portfolio, and to increase income. How these objectives can be accomplished through options trading will be described in later chapters.

There remains, however, a large body of UK investing institutions which do not deal in the options market. One reason for this is a shortage of trained staff to assume responsibility for analysing, initiating and administering transactions. If in doubt, pension fund trustees tend to shy away from such seemingly new-fangled and controversial products.

Why Should the Private Investor Trade Options?

It is, however, to individual private investors, and through their advisers (particularly stockbrokers), that LIFFE is looking to regenerate interest in individual equity options. There are several reasons why this goal is worth pursuing:

■ *Common Practice in Other Countries:* A good reason for expecting this to be a fruitful approach is that trading in equity options by the private investor is much more common in certain other stockmarkets than it is in the UK. In both the US and in Holland, for instance, retail investors account for around 70% of options turnover.

In Holland, options dealing is facilitated by banks, with quote terminals often located in local branches. In the US, investors seemingly draw little distinction between investing in options and investing in the underlying shares.

It is too simplistic to say that the level of investment in traded options is a mark of the sophistication of the private investor in the particular market concerned. To begin with, the comparison between the UK and Holland is not wholly explicable in those terms. There may be other factors which have given rise to a greater propensity to invest in equity options by individuals in these different markets.

21

■ *End of the 'Account Settlement' System:* A more likely reason why options historically have not been as widely used was the structure of the stock market itself. In London, the old system of fortnightly 'account' settlement facilitated low-cost short term trading of shares for those well enough informed to take advantage of it. This was not possible in many other markets. The advent of rolling settlement removed the scope for trading of this type. While a system of margin trading may develop (whereby shares can be dealt in by paying initially only a proportion of their cost) to offset this change, UK private investors - unlike their counterparts in the US - have traditionally been reluctant to adopt this method and may slowly be veering towards equity options as the mechanism through which such short-term trading judgements can be effected.

■ *Better Information:* one of the keys to increasing private investor interest in equity options is to raise the quality of press coverage on options and to foster the availability of options price data in the press and through other media, including the Internet. One of the most potent original generators of enquiries about equity options at LIFFE used to be the listing of options pages on CEEFAX, which began in early 1993. It was, however, discontinued some four years later, although prices are now listed on the Sky News teletext service in more detail. The interest generated by the original CEEFAX displays did, however, illustrate the underlying demand to learn about the equity and index options markets, a demand now being accommodated by the Exchange's programme of courses and other investor education.

■ *Better Informed Stockbrokers:* one aspect of this has been to enlarge the interest of the private client stockbroking community in options. This has not always been easy. Many smaller broking firms are conservatively-run and have instinctively shied away from options as being too speculative, or have become interested in them only to the extent of facilitating their clients' wishes. Option trades are viewed as relatively costly and administratively complex. Options have therefore not generally been actively promoted as a normal part of portfolio investment, or as instruments that are regularly used by private investors in other countries.

LIFFE has also stepped up its communication to private client brokers to make such firms aware that there is viable business to be done through stimulating legitimate and appropriate private investor participation in the options market. Private client brokers have also been offered extensive advice about the technical background required to provide a more comprehensive service.

A further goal is eventually to extend this educational process down the line to banks and building societies' retail networks, as happens in the equivalent institutions in other markets.

Options, Risk and Reward
It should become clear from reading this book that equity and index options are not casino-style markets in which private investors will inevitably lose money.

The options market is concerned with the management of risk. The most prominent users of both markets are companies and institutional investors among whose objectives are to hedge against the possibility of an unexpected movement in the underlying market. A hedge is a low-cost transaction which has a counteracting effect to a purchase or sale in the underlying instrument.

An investing institution, for example, might have sold its entire shareholding in Marks & Spencer because it feels the company's results, due in a month's time, will be disappointing. But its fund managers may want to be covered in case this judgement proves wrong. The options market can be used to provide such 'insurance'. If the shares go up, rather than down, the options transaction will compensate for the extra profit foregone on the earlier sale of the shares. The option can either be exercised, re-establishing the underlying holding, or else a trading profit can be booked.

To use the word 'insurance' in this context is important. Insurance is simply a means of transferring risk from one party to another. In the domestic insurance area, the risk is moved from the person who owns a house or a car to the insurance company. As with insurance, the buyer of an option pays a premium. Rather than making a claim, in the case of options the 'insurance' pay-out is the offsetting profit on the option transaction if the unexpected occurs.

By providing a means by which options can be exchanged and correctly priced, equity and index option markets provide a mechanism for absorbing risk. If insurance did not exist as a concept, economic activity would suffer. Equally in the options market, because for every buyer of an option there is an equivalent seller, the overall amount of risk is not increased. But the system's capacity to absorb risk has been improved. This must be of benefit and can scarcely be described as the workings of a casino.

What needs to be very clearly understood by the potential investor in the options market, however, is that options have quite different characteristics to ordinary shares and should be bought and sold using different techniques. To regard options as simply a geared way of profiting from a movement in the price of the underlying security is to court disaster.

Equally, option transactions should not be viewed in isolation. One deal may

23

result in a substantial profit, the next in a loss. What should be measured is the overall return at the end of a fixed period and how this would have compared, in terms of dealing costs and interest costs and savings, with conducting the transactions in the equivalent number of underlying ordinary shares.

Summary

1. Options come in a variety of forms. Call options confer the right (but not the obligation) to buy a specified number of shares at the exercise price. Put options confer the right, but not the obligation, to sell.

2. Options can be bought and sold during their life, or exercised. It is not necessary to own the underlying shares in order to buy or sell an option.

3. For every buyer of a call or put option there is someone taking the opposite stance. This counterpart is known as the 'writer' of the option.

4. Trading in options by private investors is commonplace in a number of world stockmarkets. It is becoming more common in the UK with the introduction of rolling settlement and the disappearance of the Stock Exchange 'account' system.

5. Options are available on over 70 shares and on the FTSE 100 Index.

6. One attraction of equity options is that they entail lower dealing costs than the underlying shares they represent. They are more volatile than ordinary shares, but offer the prospect of correspondingly greater returns.

7. Equity options can be used as 'insurance' by providing an offset to a transaction in the underlying shares.

8. Used correctly, options are a flexible tool for managing risk. However, option positions must be closely monitored and a disciplined approach must be adopted.

TWO

OPTION TERMINOLOGY, PRICING AND DEALING

The table of key words and definitions for this chapter can be found on page 26. Having examined the background to the concept of options, what advantages does the equity and index options market at LIFFE provide for the investor?

Earlier, we drew the distinction between traditional options and traded options, or equity options as they are now more normally known. Among the drawbacks of buying options through the traditional options market are illiquidity, the market's comparatively unstructured nature, and the fact that these options can only be exercised with the original seller.

Each of these disadvantages is avoided by using equity options. This applies whether they are those available at LIFFE, or on any other regulated options exchange around the world.

The main characteristics of exchange-traded options and the advantages to investors who use them can be listed as follows:

■ *Centralised Trading:* the advantage of trading being centralised in one market, whether a physical one or an electronic one, is self evident. The market provides a place where buyers and sellers can meet physically or interact electronically, without dealings being fragmented. Investors and market participants, in London and elsewhere, have now become quite used to a market existing only in electronic format. The London Stock Exchange's introduction of an electronic order book to replace some of the dealings previously conducted by telephone is one example of this revolution and, while some large exchanges still have a physical trading floor, this is now considered less essential than it once was for the operation of an efficient, well-regulated market. This is especially true in situations (like equity options) where large numbers of instruments are traded with fluctuating and sometimes quite low levels of volume in each one at any one time. Electronics is well suited to a situation like this, and LIFFE is planning to replace its current floor based equity options market with an electronic, screen-based one in November 1998.

■ *A Standardised and Structured Market:* One way in which traded equity options differ from traditional options is that contract size and other related parameters are standardised. The market has a coherent structure. The advantage of this is that a common specification of this sort makes comparisons across different options easier. It also improves liquidity, the ease with which buying and selling can take place, by focusing the terms of the options on specific points known in advance.

KEY TERMINOLOGY

Intrinsic Value - the amount by which the price of the underlying shares is above (in the case of a call) or below (in the case of a put) the exercise price of the option.

Time Value - the difference between the price of an option and its intrinsic value (if any). Time value falls away progressively as an option approaches expiry.

In-the-money Option - an option with some intrinsic value

At-the-money Option - an option whose strike price roughly equates to the price of the underlying shares.

Out-of-the-money Option - an option with no intrinsic value. The price consists solely of time value, which will fall as the option approaches expiry.

Margin - funds which an option writer must deposit with his broker to ensure that he is financially capable of meeting the cost involved if the option is exercised against him.

Volatility - a statistical measure of past fluctuations in the price of the underlying shares. Generally speaking, the more volatile a share, the higher will be the price of its options. Volatility, however, itself fluctuates over time and increasing or decreasing volatility can either offset or reinforce movements in the price of an option taking place for other reasons.

■ *The number of stocks on which options are available is restricted to those the exchange can be reasonably sure will generate a good level of two-way trade:* Option stocks are occasionally phased out if insufficient demand is present. The introduction of new options series, say as a result of a marked change in the underlying share price, is done on the basis of known and predetermined criteria. Even allowing for this management of trading liquidity, there are many options series which from time to time become infrequently traded. An additional advantage of a centralised and structured market is that the market-makers assigned to quote prices in these options must quote a two-way price at all times. This enables the small investor in particular to deal in even the most illiquid options.

■ *Competitive price formulation:* Prices are arrived at in the market (be it floor based or electronic) through the competitive interaction of buyers and sellers and, in the case of an electronic market, the operation of an electronic order book. This helps to ensure that prices always reflect reasonably accurately their true underlying value.

■ *Transparency of Prices and Trade Information:* In addition, the exchange provides the means by which market prices are continuously and instantaneously disseminated to market users. This facilitates the monitoring and managing of options trades. Option prices are available on Sky Text, where they are updated regularly and, for those with Internet connections, several sites on the world wide web (including LIFFE's own) also disseminate periodically updated prices free of charge. These are examined in more detail in Chapter 11. Real time price services, such as Datastream/ICV's 'Market Eye', also disseminate LIFFE options price to private investors, although charges are significant for this up-to-the-minute data. Datastream/ICV can be contacted on 0171-398-1000.

LIFFE also provides a valuable function in publishing information on trading volumes and other parameters to aid decision-making by investors. These are made available to all users of the market in a timely fashion, published on LIFFE's web site, and also available through the Exchange's printed material.

■ *Regulation:* LIFFE is a Recognised Investment Exchange (RIE) under the terms of the Financial Services Act 1986 and, as such, provides extensive regulatory safeguards for its users. These ensure that the integrity of the market is fully protected.

The sophisticated nature of the market and its settlement procedures means that surveillance of exchange members' actions is made easier. Clear computer 'audit trails' for each trade conducted through the exchange can be identified.

Basic Options Terminology
Before looking in more detail at how the market works, it is necessary to get to grips with the basic terminology of options. As explained earlier, an option confers the right, but not the obligation, to buy or sell a parcel of shares at a fixed price from the present time up to a fixed date in the future.

If it is attractive to use that right (that is, if the price of the underlying share moves beyond the fixed 'exercise' price plus the cost of the option), then either the option may be capable of being sold at a profit, or alternatively it can be exercised. If not, since there is no obligation entailed in holding an option, it can be allowed to lapse. In any event the original cost of the option (or premium) is forfeited by the buyer.

Equity options differ from traditional options in that they can be bought or sold on LIFFE, offering a greater degree of choice for the holder. They can be sold prior to exercise, exercised, or allowed to lapse depending on the circumstances.

Options contracts, normally denominated in lots of 1000 shares, move in a well-defined way relative to changes in the price of the underlying shares on which they are based. In broad terms, a particular change in the price of the share will lead to a disproportionate, but statistically predictable, percentage move in the price of the option. Although this sounds simple, the process of determining how an option's price will move in different circumstances is a complex one.

An option is also more valuable the further away it is from expiry, since there is a greater probability that a potentially profitable movement in the underlying share will occur in time for the investor to take advantage of it. The price of an option reflects therefore, among other things, the relationship between the price of the underlying shares, the time remaining to expiry, and the volatility of the underlying shares.

Bearing all this in mind, the following is some basic options terminology....
The first important distinction to make is between 'calls' and 'puts'.

A **call option** gives the holder the right, but not the obligation, to buy a particular security at a fixed price up to a certain date in the future, after which time the option expires.

A **put option** gives the holder the right, but not the obligation, to sell a particular security at a fixed price up to a certain date in the future, after which time the option expires.

These terms are used in all options markets.

Calls and **puts** behave differently for a given movement in the underlying share price. If the share price goes up, the price of the call option will generally go up, because the fixed-price 'option to buy' becomes more valuable. Likewise because the put option confers the right to sell the shares at a particular price, its price will generally only rise if the underlying shares fall in value. On an upward move in the shares, a put option should normally fall in price.

In other words, call options move in the same direction as the underlying share price, put options in the opposite direction as is shown in the diagram below.

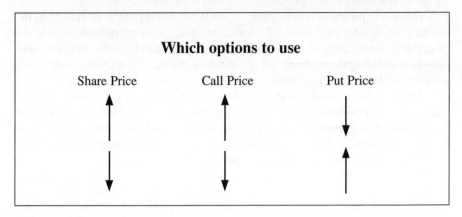

Figure 1: Which options to use.

In simple trades the private investor will be backing his or her judgement of the likely movement in the price of a particular share by buying either call options or put options. Calls will be bought if it is thought that the price of the shares is going to rise. Puts will be bought if it is thought that the price of the shares is likely to fall during the life of the option.

For each holder of an option there must be someone who is prepared to take the opposite tack. While an option buyer acquires the right but not the obligation to take a particular course of action, it follows that the person on the other side of the transaction assumes the obligation but not the right.

This person is known as the **'writer'**. The liability that the writer takes on is the obligation to make or take delivery of the underlying stock if the option is eventually exercised by the holder. Just as the buyer of the option is calculating that the underlying share price will move by sufficient to more than offset the cost of the option, the writer is expecting that it will not.

Although the term **'writer'** suggests the physical drawing up of a contract, in fact a writer is simply an options trader whose initial transaction is on the selling side rather than the buying side. Writing options is not, as is commonly assumed, necessarily an inappropriate and risky strategy for the private investor. But it is important that the investor should understand prior to entering a transaction exactly what risk it entails. In the case of strategies involving writing options, this is explained further in Chapter Six.

For assuming his obligations, however, the writer does get a reward. The writer retains the option **'premium'**. The premium is, in effect, the price of the option (call or put) to the buyer. This cost, together with related dealing expenses, is foregone by the option buyer in all circumstances.

The option premium is determined according to supply and demand within the market, but also by reference to the time remaining to expiry and the price of the underlying shares relative to the **exercise, or strike price,** of the option. Other factors influencing the premium are interest rates, the incidence of dividends on the underlying shares, and how volatile or otherwise are the underlying shares.

Although the premium is determined by the interaction of buyers and sellers in the market, it is likely that it will correspond closely to the fair value ascribed to it by a standard mathematical pricing model. Such models weigh and balance the factors mentioned above according to proven mathematical relationships. Computer software is available at low cost to perform this function.

Exercising options and their expiry dates are also complex subjects in themselves. **Exercise** is defined as the use of the right by the option holder to purchase the shares at the exercise price if the option is a call, or to sell the underlying shares at the exercise price if the option is a put. Equity options traded on LIFFE are termed 'American-style' exercise. This means that they can be exercised at any time up to expiry. The alternative 'European-style' exercise convention limits the right to exercise to the expiry date alone.

When a call is exercised the writer of the option is obliged to make delivery of the underlying shares at the exercise price, and the holder of the option is obliged to take delivery.

When a put is exercised, the writer is obliged to take delivery of the underlying shares at the exercise price and the holder of the option is obliged to make delivery.

In both cases it is necessary for the deliverer of stock to ensure that he has the stock available to fulfil the terms of the contract, while the receiver of stock must ensure that he has the cash available to pay for it on the basis of the price implied in the option contract.

In order to ensure that the necessary funds are in place, a system of deposits known as **'margin'** is operated. Margin requirements are funds or collateral that an option writer must maintain on deposit with his stockbroker to assure his ability to fulfil his financial obligations under the options contract. Buyers of equity options (whether calls or puts), because they pay the option premium at the outset, have no further financial obligations and are not therefore subject to margin requirements.

However, if an option holder exercises his right to acquire the underlying shares, he then becomes subject to the margin requirements applicable to the shares concerned from the time the option is exercised until the transaction in the underlying equity is settled after ten trading days.

Option Expiry Cycles

The **expiry** of options is carefully co-ordinated to ensure that these events take place evenly through the year. Options are normally created on the basis of one of three different expiry cycles, each of which will have three separate expiry months quoted at any one time. Thus one cycle will have options expiring in January, April, July and October, another in February, May, August and November and the third in March, June, September and December. With three of these four expiry months available at any time, each share on which options are available should have three option expiry dates stretching forward up to a maximum of nine months in the future.

When one option expiry date passes, a new set of options is created for the most distant next expiry month in the cycle. Equity option expiry dates are determined in advance and are normally the third Wednesday in the month. Expiry of index options takes place on a different day, normally the third Friday of the month.

In addition to the three different expiry dates for the call and put options on each underlying security, each option category has several different option series based around differing exercise prices.

An option **series** is simply another name for a specific class of option. Thus the widget-maker XYZ plc whose underlying shares are priced at 260p, might have options available with strike prices of 220p, 240p, 260p, 280p and 300p for March, June and September expiry. Hence there would be 15 different call options available and 15 corresponding put options, 30 options series in all. The March 260 calls would be one option series, the March 260 puts another, and so on.

The number of options series for each company is effectively determined by the movement in the underlying share price. Except at the expiry date, when ten series (five calls and five puts) based on the new expiry month are automatically created, new options series (ie. a call and put with a new exercise price) are generally introduced if the underlying share price moves outside the price range represented by existing options series and stays there for a specified length of time.

The intervals between exercise prices are determined by the underlying share price on the basis of a predetermined formula. Broadly speaking, the higher the price of the underlying security, the greater the interval between exercise prices. Hence a stock priced at 240p would have options series with strike prices at 200p, 220p, 240p, 260p, and so on, whereas a stock priced at 550p would have options series exercisable at 50p intervals - at 500p, 550p, 600p, 650p, and so on.

Depending on the movement in the underlying price, each share upon which options are listed will have a varying number of series available. Stable shares will tend to have fewer than more volatile ones. Other things being equal, those series furthest from the exercise price will tend to be less actively traded - unless the share price is moving rapidly in their direction. Those with less time to expiry tend to be more actively traded than those that are 'longer-dated'.

The reasoning behind the offering of a choice of different exercise prices for each option stock is so that options with different characteristics are created for each security. These are normally known as **in-the-money, at-the-money**, and **out-of-the-money** options. The concept is intuitively easiest to understand in the case of call options. In this case, **in-the-money** options are those where the price of the underlying shares stands significantly above the exercise price of the option. This means that the option has some intrinsic value, since the contract could be exercised immediately and the resulting shares sold for a profit.

At-the-money options are those whose exercise price is the same as or close to the market price of the underlying shares. **Out-of-the-money** options are those where the exercise price (in the case of the calls) significantly exceeds the price of the underlying shares. Thus in the case of XYZ plc above, with the underlying share price at 260p, the 240 calls are in-the-money to the tune of 20p (ie the strike price is 20p below the price of the shares), the 260 calls are at-the-money and the 280 calls are out-of-the-money. Here the exercise price is 20p more than the price of the shares.

In the case of put options the concept is reversed. Puts are in-the-money if the exercise price is above the current underlying share price and out-of-the-money if the exercise price is below the underlying share price.

The Components of Options Prices

The concept of whether or not options are in-the-money or out-of-the-money is inextricably linked to the price (or premium) of the option. As can be seen from *Figure 2* on page 33, which gives examples of real options prices, even options which are significantly out-of-the- money may have a market value.

Let's take the July 1200 calls as an example. The price is 52-59, a mid-price of 55 $1/_2$p. But since the share price, at 1138p is some 62p under the exercise price, the option has no intrinsic value. That is, if the shares remained unchanged until April, the option would expire worthless. There would be no point exercising the option, because the share could be bought at a lower price in the market.

The price of 55 $1/_2$p therefore represents the time-value of the option. This is the market's assessment of the value of the probability that the shares will rise above the 1200 strike price in the remaining months of the option's life. The October 1200 calls, with a mid-price of 81 $1/_2$p, are still out-of-the-money, but have longer to run and, therefore, a higher time value. This is because the probability of being able to sell or exercise the option at a profit in the intervening period is higher - simply because there is a longer time period in which the required movement in the underlying shares could take place.

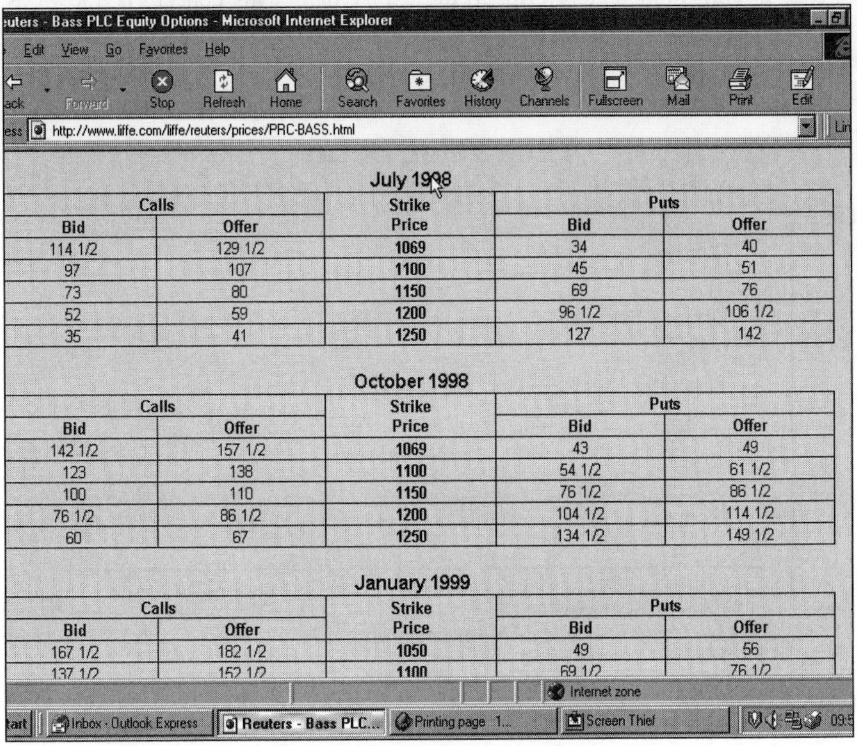

July 1998

Calls		Strike Price	Puts	
Bid	Offer		Bid	Offer
114 1/2	129 1/2	1069	34	40
97	107	1100	45	51
73	80	1150	69	76
52	59	1200	96 1/2	106 1/2
35	41	1250	127	142

October 1998

Calls		Strike Price	Puts	
Bid	Offer		Bid	Offer
142 1/2	157 1/2	1069	43	49
123	138	1100	54 1/2	61 1/2
100	110	1150	76 1/2	86 1/2
76 1/2	86 1/2	1200	104 1/2	114 1/2
60	67	1250	134 1/2	149 1/2

January 1999

Calls		Strike Price	Puts	
Bid	Offer		Bid	Offer
167 1/2	182 1/2	1050	49	56
137 1/2	152 1/2	1100	69 1/2	76 1/2

Figure 2: Option prices as quoted on LIFFE's web site.

Now let's look at the July 1100 calls. Here the option is the in-the-money to the tune of 38p (the share price of 1138p less the strike price of 1100p), but the mid-price of the options is 102p. This means that the option's price (or premium) is made up of an intrinsic value of 38p and time value of 64p (the premium of 102p minus the intrinsic value of 38p). Similarly, for the October 1100 calls, the intrinsic value is the same (38p) but the time value is higher at $92\frac{1}{2}$ p (mid-price of $130\frac{1}{2}$p minus intrinsic value unchanged at 38p). The time value is, therefore, the amount by which an option's price exceeds its intrinsic value (if any).

Just as the time-value increases the longer different options have to run, so the passage of time means that the time-value of a given option will decrease the nearer it gets to expiry. The time-value of an option is not a constant amount.

For any given underlying price, therefore, the time-value of, say, a July call (or put) will be lower at the beginning of July - three weeks before expiry - than it will be, say, at the end of April - three months before expiry. It will gradually decrease to zero immediately prior to the expiry date. This concept is known as **time value decay**. The normal pattern of time value delay is shown in the diagram below.

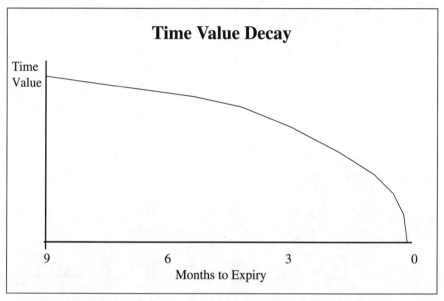

Figure 3: Time Value Decay.

Because what governs the attractiveness and potential profitability of options is the likelihood or otherwise of significant movement in the share price, a concept central to the valuation and analysis of options is volatility.

Volatility should be intuitively quite easy to grasp. It is, however, often something that even experienced investors find confusing.

Every investor knows that there are some shares that move around more violently than others. Equally there are times when an individual share goes through a quiet period, when little movement occurs in its price, and it then subsequently explodes into life.

Volatility is normally expressed as the percentage band inside which the share price would be expected to remain two–thirds of the time throughout a one–year period. A share with volatility of 20% standing at 100p would therefore expect to see its share price fluctuate between 80p and 120p – with only a one–in–three chance of moving outside these bands.

The next step is to appreciate that the more volatile a particular share, then (other things being equal) the higher will be the price of any given option relating to it.

Why should this be so? The reason is an obvious one. The greater the volatility, the more likely it is that a move will occur during the life of the option which will enable the holder to sell or exercise at a profit. The option writer will therefore want to be compensated for this additional risk through receiving a higher premium at the outset.

So far so good. The next complication is that past share price performance may not be a reliable guide to the future. The statistical techniques described above measure volatility based on the past performance of a particular share. This is known as **historic volatility**. It is typically calculated on the basis of share prices over a period corresponding to the remaining life of the option. Historic volatility for an option with three months to run might be worked out using the daily share price data over the last three months, for instance.

What option buyers and writers are interested in, however, is not what has happened in the past, but the expected future trend in volatility, or **expected volatility**.

And there is another complication. While the historic volatility of a particular share can be calculated from its past price history, the price of a particular option in the market may suggest a different figure. The level of an option's premium, when run through a pricing model, will give a clue as to the level of volatility the market is pricing into its calculations at any one time. This is known as **implied volatility**. Deciding whether a particular option is attractive will depend upon one's own view of volatility.

The important point to remember here is that implied volatility can change sharply over time for a variety of reasons, including market factors and events relating to the underlying shares. Changes in volatility can therefore either reinforce or dampen down changes in option prices occurring as a result of the other variables outlined.

Another factor of significance in determining an option's premium is the level of interest rates. This is because buying call options, rather than the equivalent quantity of underlying shares, entails a significantly lower capital outlay and leaves cash free to be invested elsewhere.

High rates of interest increase the attractiveness of call options to buyers and hence tend to inflate call option premiums. The reverse is true in the case of puts. It is the general level of interest rates rather than specific changes in rates which has the effect on options premiums, since the mix of strike prices and expiry dates means that the impact of changes in rates is gradually priced into option premiums along with all the other factors involved.

The same is true of dividends on the underlying shares. Holders of call and put options are not entitled to receive dividends on the underlying shares. Although this would suggest that call option premiums would fall sharply when the underlying shares go ex-dividend (when the market price of the shares is adjusted to reflect the imminent payment of a dividend), this tends not to happen. Dividend payment dates, the amount of dividends and ex-dividend dates are all known well in advance and tend automatically to be reflected in the prices of the options in the days and weeks leading up to the date.

The impact of changes in the various main components of an option's price (or premium) is summarised in *Figure 4* below.

Premium Movement Trends

	Call premium	Put premium
Rise in underlying share price	Rise	Fall
Fall in underlying share price	Fall	Rise
Increase in market volatility	Rise	Rise
Longer time to expiry	Rise	Rise
Interest rate rise	Rise	Fall
Higher dividend yield	Fall	Rise

Figure 4: Effect of changes to components of option prices.

How the Market Functions

From the investor's standpoint, a prerequisite for dealing in equity options is a clear understanding of the nature of options, the types of strategies that can be used and their profit and loss potential. It is also necessary to have a good relationship with a stockbroker sympathetic to the idea of trading options – if you are new to option trading then perhaps one who can offer advice on dealing procedures, suggest opportunities for profitable strategies, highlight market anomalies and perhaps provide research and analysis.

Familiarity with contract specifications: size; strike price; expiry; exercise and settlement; minimum price changes and so on is also essential. Most equity options contracts on LIFFE are based on units of 1,000 shares and the various parameters of a typical options contract are summarised in *Figure 5* on page 37.

Equity Option Contract Specification

Unit of trading	One option normally equals rights over 1000 shares.
Expiry months	January Cycle (J): means the three nearest expiry months from Jan, Apr, Jul, Oct cycle. February Cycle (F): means the three nearest expiry months from Feb, May, Aug, Nov cycle. March Cycle (M): means the three nearest expiry months from Mar, Jun, Sep, Dec cycle.
Exercise/Settlement day	Exercise by 17.20 on any business day, extended to 18.00 for all series on a Last Trading Day. Settlement Day is six business days after the day of Exercise/Last Trading Day.
Last Trading Day	16.10* Third Wednesday of the Expiry Month.
Quotation	pence/share.
Minimum Price Movement (Tick size and value)	0.5 pence/share. (£5.00)
Trading hours	08.35 - 16.10*

Contract Standard

Delivery will be 1000 shares (or other such number of shares as determined by the terms of the contract).

Option Premium

Premium is payable in full by the buyer on the business day following a transaction.

Exercise Price and Exercise Price Intervals

Pence, eg. 240, 260, 280. The interval between Exercise Prices is set according to a fixed scale determined by the Exchange.

Introduction of new Exercise Prices

Additional Exercise Prices will be introduced on the business day after the underlying share price has exceeded the second highest, or fallen below the second lowest, available Exercise Price.

* Commencement of Closing Rotation

Figure 5: An example of a standard equity option specification.

The option market at LIFFE is currently conducted on the floor of the exchange in trading pits, although this system will be replaced from November 1998 by electronic trading for individual equity options. The pits are are separate areas of the market floor devoted to trading in particular groups of options. The system through which prices are made and deals done is known as 'open outcry'. This is a market mechanism whereby a 'crowd' of dealers in the pit conducts a continuous open auction, shouting bids and offers at each other and trading on them as appropriate, according to preset rules.

The crowd of dealers in the pit at any one time will contain the official market-makers in the particular equity options concerned, floor dealers from a variety of member firms acting for both clients and on their own account. Others present will be independent traders known as 'locals', and Exchange officials monitoring the market to make sure that no irregularities occur. The Exchange officials are also there to see that the market remains orderly, to ensure that any limit orders are executed if appropriate, and to input price changes into the Exchange's data capture systems.

Communication between dealers in the pits is through voice and hand signals. Dealers signal the results of their trades to their booths on the floor of the market. The details of the deal are then relayed by telephone to the stockbroker's front office and reported back to the client.

Hence the typical order process in a floor trading environment runs as follows:

1. Client calls broker with option order.
2. Broker relays order to firm's trading floor booth through voice link.
3. Booth signals to pit trader or passes him order slip.
4. Pit trader executes order and signals back confirmation.
5. Booth confirms the order execution to front office.
6. Front office reports to client.

Although there are six distinct steps in this process, the time elapsing while this is done will often only be a matter of a few seconds.

After the deal.....
Once orders representing a purchase by one party and a sale by another have been executed, the trade details are matched and registered. Buyers of options, both calls and puts, are required to pay the full premium amount to their LIFFE member on the business day following the execution of the order.

In turn that same morning the LIFFE member must make this payment to his 'clearing member', or direct to the London Clearing House (LCH) if he is a clearing member, and the same day LCH will then pay the premium to the clearing member through which the sale was made for onward transmission to the writer of the option contract.

Option writers are required at all times to maintain sufficient cash funds or other acceptable collateral to assure contract performance. These margin requirements are determined by the LIFFE member acting as immediate principal to the writer of the contract and must at a minimum be equal to the margin requirements of the Clearing House.

Options are exercised by the holder submitting an exercise notice to his LIFFE member who in turn gives notice of exercise, through his clearing member. Through a system of random allocation, LCH will then issue a notice, to another clearing member who is the writer of an identical option that is being called upon, to fulfil the obligations of the options contract. The clearing member will in turn randomly assign the notice down to the next level in the chain. In practice all a private investor will need to do is communicate to his stockbroker the instruction to exercise the option.

Underlying equity bargains which arise as a result of the exercise of an equity option are processed through the London Stock Exchange settlement system in the normal way.

Summary

1. An advantage of dealing in exchange-traded options is that trading is conducted on a structured and centralised market. Prices are arrived at through the competing actions of buyers, sellers and market-makers, and are widely disseminated. The market is a regulated one.

2. The price (or premium) of an option, which is paid by the buyer to the writer, is determined in the market by reference to a number of different variables. These are chiefly the price of the underlying shares, the time remaining to expiry, and the volatility of the underlying shares.

3. The volatility of the underlying shares governs how probable or otherwise it will be for the holder of an option to exercise at a profit. Similar options on volatile shares therefore tend to have higher prices than those on less volatile shares, other things being equal.

4. Volatility can vary significantly over time. Fully understanding all the detailed aspects of volatility is not the be-all and end-all of dealing in options, but it is important in the context of some types of option trades. Historic and implied volatility calculations are normally generated by easy-to-use computer software.

5. Options can be in-the-money, out-of-the-money, or at-the-money. This is determined by the position of the exercise price relative to the price of the underlying shares. Option prices reflect the value placed on the remaining time to expiry, and any intrinsic value which the option may possess.

6. Time value present in an option erodes at an increasingly rapid rate the closer the option gets to expiry.

7. Option trading in London is currently conducted through the system of floor trading known as 'open outcry'. However, screen-based trading of equity options is due to begin in November 1998.

THREE

CHOOSING A STOCKBROKER

This chapter explains how to go about choosing a broker to deal in equity and index options. The table of key words and definitions for this chapter can be found on page 42.

For various reasons mentioned earlier, some stockbrokers are reluctant to deal in traded options for their clients. The experienced private investor wishing to deal in options may therefore have to use a different broker to his or her normal one.

So, if the investor finds that his or her broker does not offer an options service, or does not offer the level of advice felt to be needed for equity and index options dealing and administration, what is the best way to go about selecting one who does?

A list of private client brokers offering an options service is available from LIFFE, Cannon Bridge, London EC4R 3XX. Before turning to the question of how to pick a broker from this list, it is first worth looking at why certain brokers are reluctant to deal in equity options for private investors.

Brokers and Options

Some of the reasons are sound business concerns, but generally they reflect some of the myths and prejudices which have grown up around the options market. The most common are:

■ *Options are expensive:* some brokers with responsibility for managing private client money consider options expensive. Most private investors will initially, and quite properly, want their initial participation in the options market to be relatively small, perhaps no larger in underlying terms than the normal parcel of shares in which they would expect to deal. Given that each contract represents 1,000 shares, this means that the broker would be dealing in perhaps no more than one or two contracts, leaving the client subject to minimum commission levels. From the standpoint of the broker, minimum commissions may be set at levels which recoup some, but not all, of the overheads involved in doing small deals. Option

---

KEY TERMINOLOGY

Execution-only - a broker who deals – usually at a lower rate – without offering advice. This type of service is most appropriate for experienced investors in options.

Dealing-with-advice - a broker who will offer advice on particular strategies and help to monitor them for the investor. Commission charges are higher, but this may be the best type of service for the first-time option investor.

Portfolio Adviser - a broker who provides, as well as a dealing facility, overall advice on the composition of a client's portfolio. The broker may be remunerated partly on a fee basis.

Discretionary Service - a service where the broker administers all aspects of the client's portfolio without prior reference to the client.

Client Agreement Form - a form which the client must complete and sign before dealing can be done. It establishes the business relationship between the broker and investor and is a regulatory requirement designed for the protection of both sides.

Dealing 'at best' - where the broker deals at the prevailing market price.

Public Limit Order - an order to buy at a specific price not currently available in the market. These orders are lodged with the Exchange and will be executed by Exchange officials if the price limits are reached within that trading day.

---

trading may therefore at best be viewed as something of a loss leader, and at worst not really worth the effort. From the standpoint of the client, however, the potential for gain if the options trade comes good may well justify the dealing costs involved.

■ *Options are administratively messy:* compared to dealing in ordinary shares, options sometimes require more administrative time. This is partly because of the margin requirements in connection with options writing and the exercise of options generally. These margin requirements entail collateral and cash to travel back and forth at specified times, together with related payments and receipts. This contrasts with ordinary share dealing where the transfer process is comparatively straightforward. The option position may need to be monitored throughout its life and the client alerted about exercise or expiry as appropriate. This gives rise, from the broker's standpoint, to additional costs in terms of staff time. Clients may also be nervous about options positions and may expect the broker to stay closely in touch, again giving rise to extra costs.

■ *Lack of qualified staff:* another problem brokers face is that of a shortage of staff familiar with options administration procedures, or qualified to advise clients on options strategies. Because of this scarcity, and the often highly complex and specialised nature of options trading and settlement, such staff tend to command above-average salaries.

■ *Options are too risky:* some brokers shun dealing in options because they perceive them to be highly speculative and risky. While it is correct to say that options are more volatile than the underlying shares on which they are based, they are much more a tool for the management of risk. In fact, a number of option strategies are more conservative than dealing directly in the underlying stock. The precise amount of capital at risk is known in advance.

Some brokers undoubtedly feel that ill-judged options trades, which result in clients losing money, may attract odium to their firms. Not unnaturally, they wish to avoid this at all costs. This problem is best addressed by more education of the stockbroking community on how to advise their clients about equity options.

■ *Options markets are unregulated casinos:* as explained earlier, this is patently incorrect. Options exchanges are closely regulated and because they offer the opportunity to reduce and manage risk, cannot be described as casinos. The fact that some investors use options to speculate on the direction of the stockmarket does not invalidate this point. The risk involved in options is known and controllable.

It is also worth remembering that market-makers in the stockmarket habitually use equity and index options as a way of 'squaring their books', in effect 'laying off' risk in much the same way as a bookmaker would.

■ *Options are too complex:* brokers sometimes do not realise that, although the mathematical concepts underlying options are complex, trading in options successfully does not require detailed mathematical knowledge. Inexpensive software packages are available which enable the pricing of options and formulation and charting of options strategies to be done with comparative ease on a standard personal computer. These can be used by both broker and client, and can be provided by the broker to the client to generate customer loyalty. The use to which these packages can be put is outlined in Chapter Eight.

For the private investor who has not used options before, all this may seem academic and irrelevant. What is required is the ability to deal in options at reasonable cost, possibly with a modicum of advice about options trading strategies as greater familiarity with the market is acquired. From the broker's standpoint, some of this information and advice can be presented in a standardised form through client newsletters, either free of charge or subscription-based.

The question brokers must ask themselves is whether the provision of such a service is something which can be neglected. This is particularly so in view of the increasing use of equity options by private individuals since the end of 'account trading' and the move to rolling settlement. The brokers who provide options dealing facilities clearly view it as a way of attracting business that can be processed economically, as well as possibly gaining new clients who will eventually move all their dealings to the firm.

Types of Stockbrokers
Over the years the image of stockbrokers has varied considerably. In the novels of Trollope and Dickens, they are presented as seedy, disreputable characters. In 1920s Wall Street, their image changed to that of hard-nosed market manipulators who preyed on unsuspecting private investors by roping them into speculative stocks while they - the professionals - sold out. In the 1950s, 1960s and 1970s stockbrokers were more likely to be seen as City fat cats in top hats and pinstripes. In the 1980s the image shifted to the 'greed is good' yuppie with the Porsche and mobile phone.

The caricatures are all no more than that. Private client stockbrokers in particular tend to be normal, professional people who have continued, through all the ups and downs of the market, to do the best for their clients by offering an informed and personal service.

This is not to say that there have been no changes to the structure of the market. One difference from the market of a decade or so ago is that many large firms decided that looking after private clients was either too costly, or too labour intensive, or both. Private client business for many may also have seemed out of step with the high-tech dealing profits and lucrative merger and acquisition fees capable of being earned elsewhere in the market.

By contrast private client stockbrokers, with some justification, regard the service they offer to their clients as the very bedrock of what stockbroking should be about.

The result of this divergence of attitudes is that many, mainly smaller, firms took the view that competing with the larger players for a share of the business dished out by institutional investors would be difficult, and decided to specialise in offering services to the private client.

A number of private client brokers have merged over the past ten years or so in order to spread the cost of investment in systems required by the new market order. One facet of the new-style electronic market in shares which was ushered in by Big Bang in 1986, for example, was that there was no pressing need for regional brokers to maintain offices in London simply to have a presence on the market floor. This has aided the process of consolidation among smaller regional firms.

The investment that firms have been obliged to make in the CREST settlement system and in connecting to the SETS trading system for the top 100 shares has hastened this consolidation.

Many regional firms, for instance, are now represented in one of the main regional financial centres together with offices in a number of adjoining provincial towns. These firms tend to retain a regional focus and personal touch, but benefit from being part of a large organisation by spreading the cost of processing and settling deals.

In addition, the idea of a low-cost, no-frills stockbroking service has also been introduced and has caught on quickly. Such firms are commonplace in the US. In Britain they have prospered to a degree from the expansion in share ownership engendered by the government's privatisation programme, and also by gaining market share from traditional brokers whose clients have become dissatisfied with high commission levels.

No-frills brokers are normally situated in low-cost locations and operate both a highly sophisticated telephone order-taking system geared to rapid throughput of orders, and streamlined settlement. Administration is simplified by having clients hold stock in a broker's nominee account, and through linking client balances to high interest bank accounts in order to avoid cheque processing.

The big structural changes in share markets since the mid-1980s have meant that the choice open to individuals looking to select a stockbroker for the first time, and indeed for existing clients of a broker who may wish to move their account, is wider now than it has ever been in the past.

The different types of service available can be briefly described as follows:

■ *Execution-only*: Though it has an ominous ring, 'execution (ie. dealing) only' broking is simply another name for the no-frills service outlined in the previous paragraphs. There are several stockbroking operations which offer no-frills dealing. An execution-only service is also offered by some High Street banks and Building Societies.

The execution-only broker offers simply a dealing service with no element of advice. On occasion some may offer research on a cash basis, provide subscription newsletters and organise seminars which investors may find useful. Frequent traders can expect commission rebates.

This type of service is popular with experienced stockmarket investors who make their own share selections and who are prepared to back their own judgement without looking for advice. Those investors looking for a father-confessor figure will get short shrift from an execution-only broker.

Others likely to use them include those whose stockmarket investment is confined to privatisations and other new issues and who may therefore occasionally have the need to sell small parcels of shares at the lowest cost possible.

Although some execution-only brokers offer an equity and index options dealing service, for reasons which will be explained later it may be best for those dealing in options for the first time to look to a broker who, while charging higher commission, may also be prepared to offer advice. Some specialist options brokers offer a choice of advisory or execution-only service.

■ *Dealing-with-advice:* this is a straightforward service obtainable from most stockbrokers other than those offering solely an execution-only facility. The idea is that commission is charged at a standard rate (more expensive than execution-only) but that a client will have a designated contact name at the firm who will deal on his or her behalf and who may be contacted on the telephone from time to time for advice.

The important point here is that the relationship should be two-way. The broker will be reluctant to spend too much time discussing ideas if deals never result from the discussions. Equally, reasonably frequent dealing may result in the broker taking a more active role by initiating ideas. Simple research may also be offered as part of the package.

The service will not, however, include any more comprehensive advice on how other aspects of the client's financial affairs should be managed, and other services (such as periodic valuations or the preparation of capital gains tax statements) may well not be available or else carry an additional charge.

■ *Portfolio advice:* the next tier of service is a more comprehensive one which entails the broker discussing with the client his objectives for the portfolio (whether maximisation of income or capital growth), other aspects of his financial affairs, and providing as a matter of course information relating to the capital gains tax position on holdings, whether to invest via a tax-efficient Personal Equity Plan, and so on. Charges may be levied via an annual fee on top of dealing commissions, and will reflect this enhanced level of service. This approach clearly involves the broker taking a more active role in the management of the client's financial affairs.

■ *Wholly discretionary:* this means that the broker makes all the decisions on behalf of the client, who is informed after the event rather than before. Some investors may find this approach rather unnerving, although a good broker operating in this way should be able to offer a performance from the client's portfolio better than the individual could have managed on his or her own.

Remuneration for the broker for this type of service is more likely to be in the form of a percentage annual fee linked to the value of the portfolio. If the portfolio enjoys good appreciation, the broker's fee will rise - a worthwhile incentive and one which the investor should feel happy to accept.

Which to Choose?

It will probably be apparent that, whatever type of broking service an individual has for his or her dealings in ordinary shares, that service may not be appropriate for trading equity and index options.

The complexity of the options market and the need for the close monitoring of some option positions means for example that, for the relatively inexperienced options trader, an execution-only service may not be appropriate.

Although an execution-only broker should advise the client about technicalities such as expiry dates and exercise, the first-timer may well feel the need for a little hand-holding which an execution-only broker will not provide.

At the other end of the scale, it may take a brave individual to hand over discretion to a broker to manage an option portfolio, even though discretionary brokers are bound to act within the parameters set by the client.

The dealing-with-advice service may be the best to use until the individual gains sufficient confidence to formulate trading strategies independently and do all the necessary things to monitor their progress.

As outlined above, however, it is possible that the individual's existing broker is one of those for whom options are a closed book and whose firm does not yet offer an options dealing service. This means that a new broker must be chosen specifically for options dealing. It may be worthwhile the individual checking with his or her existing broker before making the change, however. More brokers are tending to offer an options trading service, and these numbers may increase as LIFFE's efforts to educate the private client broking community continue.

Armed with the still comparatively short list of brokers which offer trading facilities for private investors in options, the process of choosing an options broker is somewhat similar to the process of choosing a broker for ordinary share dealing.

The Selection Process
Some people find a broker through a personal recommendation from a friend, accountant, solicitor, or financial adviser. However, such recommendations are subjective. Particularly in an area as specialised as options, it is important for the investor to make the right choice and exercise his or her own judgement as to which broker might be best for these purposes.

Although it is perfectly possible these days to find a stockbroker simply by consulting the telephone directory or Yellow Pages, this can be haphazard and might, in any event, only give a local list. In contrast to the situation of a few years ago, brokers are now free to advertise and many of the larger ones, particularly the execution-only firms, do just that. Consulting the *Financial Times* and magazines such as the *Investors Chronicle* should yield a satisfactory number of names and telephone numbers.

Armed with these aids, the potential options investor can begin compiling a short list. A standard letter to each is probably the best approach to take. Telephoning stockbrokers can be a confusing experience for the new client, and establishing the ground rules in writing at the outset - what type of service is required, what further information is needed and so on - is important. The letter should mention traded options specifically, and request a face-to-face meeting.

It is not, however, necessary to chose a broker close at hand. Modern communications and the way the market is organised means that all brokers have instant access to the same information. Choosing a local broker who happens to be a golf chum is, however, to risk personal feelings getting the way of making money - the object of the whole exercise. Judgement and advice needs to be impartial, not influenced by any thoughts of personal upset or animosity.

Another positive aspect about requesting information from a broker is that almost all will send, along with a brochure, a form which will attempt to determine the investor's overall net worth and chosen investment strategies. It is an advantage for the broker to be able to know these in advance, and filling out such a form will help to crystallise these parameters and objectives in the investor's mind at the outset.

In addition, LIFFE produces a list of those brokers prepared to trade in options on behalf of private clients, listing their commission charges, contact details and other relevant information. Before contacting one, however, it is worth running through a mental checklist to decide whether or not trading in options is really for you and what type of service you require from a broker.

A Private Investor Checklist
1. Do I already deal in shares?
   If no, then options are not yet for you. It is important to be familiar with investing in ordinary shares before investing in options.

2. Should I deal in options anyway?
    This depends on your financial circumstances and temperament. Like shares, the value of options can go up and down. Options are more volatile than ordinary shares.If you are too busy to monitor options investments closely, think again.

3. Am I computer literate and interested in share price charts?
    Computer valuation techniques and the analysis of share price charts can be of considerable help in trading options. It is useful for you to know your way around a keyboard and if possible to have access to share pricing charting software. The Internet is also an extremely useful resource for would-be option traders.

4. Do I have an existing portfolio of shares in large companies?
    If yes, more complex options strategies are possible. If no, options are still a viable investment choice.

5. Does my existing broker offer an options service?
    If yes, does the service seem to be what I am looking for, or would I benefit from exploring the possibility of dealing elsewhere specifically for options?

6. If I choose a new broker, will I require advice and/or research?
    For new investors in options, research may be a handy way of gaining dealing confidence.

7. Am I prepared to give my broker discretion?
    For options trading, most investors should want to 'do it themselves'.

8. Should my broker be geographically close?
    Not necessarily.

9. Do I want to deal through a large broker or a smaller one?
    Some investors prefer the more personal service of a small broker. Others feel that size and technical back-up is more important.

10. If I choose to deal through a new broker in options, am I prepared to deal in ordinary shares through the firm too?
    It may be advantageous to do so, especially if your options trading involves strategies linking simultaneous deals in options and the appropriate underlying shares.

11. Do I have a lump sum to invest?
If yes, do NOT earmark it all for the options market.

12. If so, how much will I be prepared to put in the options market?
Remember that, other things being equal, options can lose value simply with the passage of time. Also that options tend to be more volatile than ordinary shares. It is never prudent to put all your eggs in one basket. Options trading is best considered as part of a wider investment strategy.

13. Do I anticipate having other lump sums to invest in the future?
If so, when will they appear and do you feel they should be available for the option market, or for purchasing underlying shares?

14. Do I have any anticipated large expenses at known times in the future?
If so, avoid being committed to complex option trades when they are likely to crop up.

15. Am I looking for income from my investments, or capital growth?
Options can be used in ways that generate significant income.

16. Do I want my broker to handle all the record keeping or should I do some of that myself?
You should do some of it yourself. Keeping records of your transactions and monitoring their performance is an essential part of trading options.

17. What is my annual income and how secure is it?
It is unwise to commit substantial sums to the option market if you are worried about having to set money aside in case of redundancy.

18. Am I retired / in employment / self-employed?
Options may require time to devote to monitoring their progress. This may not suit those with a demanding employer.

19. Am I paying as much as I feel comfortable with into a pension scheme?
If not, why not? The return on a pension investment can be attractive and is worth further investigation.

20. Does my partner/spouse know I intend to deal in the option market?
If no, he/she should be told, in order to save subsequent recriminations if you lose money on some of your trades.

21. Does he/she understand the risks and rewards involved?
    If no, outline them to him/her.

22. What sort of character do I have? Am I cool, calm and collected, with a logical mind, or impulsive and panicky?
    If you are impulsive or panicky, dealing in options may be a mistake. If you do not know how to answer the question, the option market is an expensive place to find out. A logical and analytical brain and a facility with numbers is a useful asset when dealing in options.

What to Expect

The process of filling out this checklist should have already determined whether options are an appropriate avenue for the investor to follow. But, after contacting a selected list of brokers, what happens next?

A number of documents are likely to come back from the broker in response to the investor's enquiry.

One will be a form to fill in to establish client records for the broker to work from. This normally represents a legal agreement, a contract which the investor enters into with the broker, by virtue of becoming a client, in order that the broker can be assured of payment for transactions being undertaken and to ensure that deals go smoothly. This should only be signed when the broker has been definitely selected as the investor's final choice.

Some paperwork is also required by the various regulatory organisations covering the stock and options markets and is designed to protect the client by establishing the ground rules at the outset.

Most firms also send out an introductory brochure produced by LIFFE which outlines the rudiments of options and the terminology of the options market.

In contrast to the practice pre-'Big Bang', most firms do not require clients to be introduced to them, nor is there any requirement for a face-to-face meeting before the account is opened and dealing can take place. To some extent, the needs fulfilled by an initial meeting are covered by the relevant customer agreement forms which new clients of the firm will be asked to sign.

However, meeting the brokers on their own home ground is always a good idea. The investor may not, when dealing in options, be dealing simply with one account executive, the norm for other portfolio dealings with most brokers, but with an options specialist or a team of specialist dealers. Going to the firm's offices and meeting the individuals concerned enables the potential new client to make a better judgement about the quality of the firm and the character of the people involved, particularly if there is more than one firm to choose from.

As with dealing in ordinary shares, it is important for the investor to feel a reasonable rapport with the people involved on the traded options desk of the firm he or she expects to deal with.

The service provided by the broking firm will also vary. Clients can expect to be charged according to the type of service required, whether execution-only or dealing-with-advice. Over and above this some firms offer additional services, either free of charge or on the basis of an additional subscription. These may include booklets on options strategies, newsletters and even options pricing software.

The important point to remember, however, is that what counts in the options market is efficient dealing and good advice, rather than free gifts. Finding a broker whose operation seems efficient and professional and with whose people the investor feels comfortable should be the most important part of making the decision about which firm to choose.

How to Deal
Dealing in options is similar to dealing in ordinary shares in some respects, different in others. Option prices are quoted by market-makers on a normal two-way bid and offer basis.

When giving the order to the dealer by telephone, it is essential to know in advance and give the dealer the following information:

■ The option series to deal in. State the stock, the exercise price, the expiry month and whether the option is a call or a put. An example of the way to quote an option series to a broker is 'the ASDA July 60 calls'.

■ Whether the order is to buy or sell, or a more complex strategy.

■ The number of contracts to buy or sell. Each contract is normally equivalent to 1,000 shares. The cost of the deal is the number of underlying shares times the option's price (or premium). Thus 15 ASDA July 60 calls priced at 7p would cost 15 x 1,000 x 7p ie. £1,050.

■ Whether the deal is an opening or closing transaction.

■ Whether the order is to buy 'at best' or whether a limit is to be set, outside of which the broker should not deal. Limit orders are placed (for a small fee) on the Public Limit Order Board at LIFFE, and are executed wherever possible by Exchange officials within that same day. However, it is important to recognise if a limit order is given there is no guarantee that the order will be executed, and that if the investor changes his mind about it, the broker must be specifically instructed to withdraw it.

One difference between options and ordinary shares is that they are dealt in on the basis of cash settlement, That is, the option premium must be paid by the buyer by 10am on the day following the purchase in the market. In practice, the broker is likely to receive funds on deposit before dealing on your behalf. Commission paid to the broker is calculated in the normal way. The broker will also usually send out a contract note in the normal way giving details of the transaction; an example is shown in *Figure 6* on page 54.

Summary

1   Many brokers do not offer a traded options dealing service to their clients. It is therefore quite possible that the investor may need to deal through a new firm if he/she wishes to deal in traded options.

2   Reasons advanced for not dealing in traded options relate mainly to their administrative complexities, lack of demand, and inability to recruit suitably trained staff.

3.   LIFFE provides a list of private client brokers offering a traded options service for their clients.

4.   Determine beforehand whether what is required is a simple dealing-only service. First-time investors in options may find a service which encompasses some element of advice to be worth the extra charges involved.

5.   It is important for the investor to be methodical in choosing an options broker, shopping around for the best terms and finding a firm with which he/she has instinctive rapport.

6.   Brokers often provide options pricing and strategy evaluation software to their clients, either free or for a modest charge. Some offer newsletters, often for an additional subscription.

7.   Dealing in options is less straightforward than dealing in ordinary shares. Remember to state the option series, the number of contracts, whether the order is to buy or sell, and whether it is opening or closing. Settlement is next day and commission will be charged.

8.   Before dealing, investors should go through the checklist on pages 48 to 51 to determine whether dealing in options is suitable for their financial circumstances and temperament.

Contract Note

Client Reference:	5717169/OPT/XX3	**Subject to the rules and regulations**
Bargain/Tax Date:	31/03/98	**of the London International**
		Financial Futures and Options
Bargain Reference:	ZH9464 amended	**Exchange**

Traded Options Account

Dear

We thank you for your instructions and have sold to you as principle

Barclays PLC
CALL OPTION/APR 98/1200 (C8925387)

You have bought to open   **Expiry Date: 15/04/98**

Time	Quantity	Price	Consideration
14.53	10	13	1,300.00

Consideration	1,300.00
Commission	20.00
VAT at 17.5%	NIL
Contract Charges	15.00
Total	£1,335.00

Please check all documents to ensure we have accurately spelt your name and address and that details of the bargain we have executed for you are correct. Please inform the company of any errors. For your convenience, our terms of settlement are printed overleaf.

Yours sincerely

A member firm of the London Stock Exchange and the Securities and Futures Authority.

Figure 6: A specimen Contract Note.

FOUR

BASIC STRATEGY: TRADING RULES AND OBJECTIVES

Having looked at the underlying concepts behind equity and index options, and mastered some of the terminology, this chapter and the next two will show how this can be put into practice by using simple strategies in the options market. First, however, the key words and definitions used in this chapter are on page 56.

Most newcomers to equity options tend to start out buying a call option. There are reasons for this. First, a call option is easier to understand intuitively. If the underlying share price rises, the price of the option, other things being equal, will also rise. This is a little easier to grasp quickly than a put option, the price of which, other things being equal, rises if the underlying share price goes down.

Secondly, most private investors are probably optimists by nature - otherwise they would not be in the market in the first place. Buying a call option, in the expectation that prices will rise, is only a short step from the decision which they will have taken previously to buy particular shares for similar reasons.

In fact, for reasons explained in Chapter Six, other option strategies may prove more appropriate for newcomers to the market. Covered writing, for instance, can produce enhanced investment returns.

Initially, however, we look at the points to be considered when buying options.

The Importance of Realistic Expectations
The first and most fundamental point is that the profitability of an options purchase will only be as good as the judgement of the person instigating it. In order to determine which option is right to buy it is necessary to have a firm view about the likely price movement in the underlying stock.

For an options purchase to be successful, the investor must predict correctly:

■ the direction of the future movement in the underlying share price;

■ the extent of the move in that direction;

■ the time period within which the move is to take place.

KEY TERMINOLOGY

Fundamentals - the analysis of a company through examination of its balance sheet, profit and loss account, trading activity and the prospects for its business.

Option Delta - the expected movement in the price of an option for a 1p movement in the price of the underlying share. This will vary between 0 and 1 in the case of a call and 0 and -1 in the case of a put. The more in-the-money an option the higher its delta.

Dealing Unit - the amount of money that the investor will normally commit to a share purchase. For option purchases, the amount of capital committed should be significantly smaller than the amount that would normally be invested in a purchase of the underlying shares.

Stop-loss - an automatic trigger point at which, if reached, a share or options transaction will be closed. Because options are more volatile than ordinary shares, stop-loss points in options trades should not be too 'tight'.

If any one of these three judgements proves incorrect, then the option trade will almost certainly lose money. So it is vital that such expectations are realistic and credible. Wishful thinking should have no place in the option investor's mind.

There is another judgement to be made. Since most shares move to some degree in line with the movement in the stockmarket as a whole, some judgement must also be made about the likely future direction of the market. An investor may be right that a particular share will rise, but if the market background is adverse, the extent of the rise is likely to be limited.

Looking forward into the future there will almost certainly be a move in the share price which could result in a profit for the investor, but if this occurs after the option expires it is of no use. It is this point which catches out many new options investors.

This point is manifested in the concept of time decay. Other things being equal, options gradually lose value as they approach expiry. As illustrated in Chapter Two, the components of the price of an option include its intrinsic value, determined by the relationship between the exercise price of the option and the market price of the underlying shares, and the time value.

The time value is the price of the option minus any intrinsic value. But because the probability of a profitable move in the underlying price diminishes as the option approaches expiry, so too does the time value component in the price of the option.

Hence the underlying share price could rise but the option price remain the same if the time value component in the option's price simultaneously decreased. Decreasing time value is the main reason why many buyers of call options end up taking losses on their trades. It is probably a good argument for making one's first call option deal a reasonably long-dated, in-the-money option where the decrease in time value will be relatively slow at the outset, and where there is also some intrinsic value as a backstop against substantial loss.

So the only way to make sure that any profits generated by an options trade are maximised is for the investor to ensure that he has clearly defined objectives and, in particular, knows at what point the deal will be closed by selling the option and taking the profit (or loss).

Uses, Advantages and Drawbacks

Although option trading is popularly presented as speculative activity, this is by no means always the case.

The speculative tag often attaching to options derives mainly from the fact that options involve gearing. That is, the percentage of any move in the underlying share price results in a magnified percentage change in the price of the option.

Another way of looking at it is that, for a small outlay represented by the cost of the option, the investor is essentially buying control over a block of shares with a much greater value. Say XYZ plc's July 360 calls are priced at 30p and the underlying share price is 370p. For an outlay of £300, the purchaser of one contract is gaining exposure to 1,000 shares with a value of £3,700, more than ten times the investment made through the option.

But another way of viewing an option is as a down payment on a shareholding. As well as gearing, therefore, one objective behind buying an option can be to plan a future purchase (or fix a particular sale price, in the case of a put) of a particular stock. The investor may not have sufficient cash to make a purchase now, but knows that funds will be available in three months time. In the meantime he expects the market, and the shares in which he is interested, to rise. A call option will 'lock in' a firm price while waiting for the cash to come in to complete the purchase.

Another 'insurance policy' use of options relates to what may happen after a particular stock has been sold by the investor. It may be that a large profit has been built up on a particular share and the investor is keen to take that profit in case the market falls and the profit is subsequently reduced. But he is not strongly convinced either way that this will happen. The shares may be sold, but the investor can cover himself in case the price appreciates further by buying the equivalent number of call options at comparatively low cost, thus retaining the opportunity to benefit from a rising share price.

Buying a put implements a similar strategy if a stock has been bought after, say, a sharp downward adjustment in its price. It may bounce, but if it doesn't, and the price continues to fall, the profit on the put option will cover (wholly or in part, depending on how many contracts have been bought) the loss on the purchase beyond a certain price and for a specific period of time.

One of these three variations: options as gearing; options as a price-fixing mechanism; and options as insurance, should represent the main reasoning behind an investor's options purchase.

To sum up, the main advantages of buying options are:

■ *Limited risk:* the most that the buyer of an option can forfeit is the cost of the option, namely the premium paid at the time of purchase. There are no other obligations on the buyer. In addition the investor has the choice, if the expected price movement does not look like materialising or if circumstances change in any way, of selling the option before expiry and recouping part of the initial outlay.

■ *Virtually unlimited profit potential:* there is absolutely no upper limit to the profit potential of a call option once the price of the underlying shares rises above the exercise price plus the cost of the option. Similarly in the case of a put, once the price of the shares falls below the exercise price minus the cost of the put, the profit increases as the shares drop in price, limited only by the fact that they will not fall beyond zero.

■ *Flexibility:* as is illustrated by the examples above of the different ways in which call and put options can be used, options confer considerable flexibility on the holder. Their interchangeablility means that, if circumstances change in the course of the life of the options, additional quantities of the same option can be bought, a proportion of the position sold, or the option used as the basis for more complex strategies which may have become appropriate. Complex options strategies are discussed in more detail in Chapter Nine.

The only significant disadvantage of buying an option (although it can be a major one) is the erosion of time value alluded to earlier. At expiry the option's value will consist solely of its intrinsic value, if any.

Rules and Objectives

Setting trading objectives, formulating rules and sticking to them is important in options trading. Movements in options can be dramatic, and it is as well to have a clear view at the outset about what strategy will be pursued if a deal begins to yield a significant profit.

Many people, however, enter the market with only the vaguest of plans and are paralysed by indecision just when decisive action is called for.

The reason for this is found in the twin emotions which govern all stockmarket investors: fear and greed. If the price of the underlying stock rises sufficiently to yield a profit on the options, the investor is faced with two conflicting thoughts. Should the options be sold to nail down the profit while the going is good? Or should one continue to hold in the hope of making an even bigger profit? Selling too early could mean missing out on a really big gain.

Controlling these emotions is particularly important in the options market. Although the opportunity for profit is in theory unlimited in the case of buying calls, because of the phenomenon of time decay the possibility of losing the capital committed to the options trade is also ever present as the option moves towards expiry.

It is therefore important to have a rational basis for supposing that the stock in question is likely to rise (or fall, in the case of a put). This will be covered in more detail in Chapter Ten on using share price charts for option timing. But it is important to think through exactly how high the underlying stock might reasonably be expected to go and over what time period.

The amount of cash devoted to each options trade should be commensurate with the risk involved. It is therefore vitally important that option buyers limit their exposure to a fraction of the dealing 'unit' they would normally use. If, say, the investor is accustomed to dealing in units of £5,000, then committing more than, say, £1,000 or £1,500 to an individual options purchase is probably unwise, bearing in mind the probabilities outlined above. As with other stockmarket investments, investors should also never enter into a transaction which could entail them losing more than they can afford.

Another essential discipline is to work out in advance at what underlying share price the option would be sold. Establishing a maximum loss on the option (say half the purchase price) is also a good idea. This is a similar process to establishing a 'stop-loss' on a share but, because options are more volatile and the potential for making profits is that much greater, setting a realistically low 'out' price avoids being taken out of the option on only a small variation in the underlying stock. Nothing is more annoying than for a stop-loss to be triggered, only to see the price rebound and miss out on what could have been a very acceptable return.

It is also important to establish the upward price target in terms of the underlying stock. This is because the time value of the option will drift down towards expiry. Calculating a theoretical profit-taking price for an option in terms of anything other than the underlying stock price is therefore imprecise.

Investors should work out at the outset (ie. before dealing) what the theoretical profit on the trade would be if the stock reaches the realistically-expected price, and how that compares with the outlay involved. Establishing all the trading parameters at the outset and, most importantly, recording them somewhere, is a way of eliminating the emotion which can disrupt an investor's thought processes and lead to missed opportunities for either taking profits, or limiting losses.

Establishing these broad parameters is really only another way of saying that the option transaction should be monitored throughout its life. If the investor, or his or her broker, is unable or unwilling to monitor these positions on a constant basis, then options may not be an appropriate investment for that particular investor regardless of their other attractions. However, the availability of option prices at various web sites, on Sky Text, and on services such as 'Market Eye' means it is easier than it once was for the average investor to keep tabs on an option deal.

One of the great trading rules of the options market is that if anything causes the investor to doubt the wisdom of holding a particular option, the position should be closed without delay. **'If in doubt, get out'**. There is no point, as one might do in a stock, holding on in the hope that better times will eventually come. In a straightforward option purchase, time decay as the option moves closer towards expiry works against the holder. Ordinary shares don't expire, and therefore time does not work against them.

Above all it is important not to stick too dogmatically to a particular stance in the market. Although it is always wise to establish the trading parameters which will govern the decision-taking process, these parameters should not be adhered to willy-nilly if circumstances change. If the outlook for a particular stock appears to have improved (results are better than expected; there are rumours of takeover in the offing; or a bid is announced) it may be wise to abandon a previous profit 'lock-in' point and institute a higher one. The same thing works in reverse if the fundamentals for the company worsen. It pays to be flexible.

For the few trades that go spectacularly right, many will be unexciting. The aim of all trading is to minimise the losses that occur when things go wrong and to maximise the profits of the ones which succeed. Cutting losses relatively quickly is a vital element in this.

Last but not least, much can be learnt from studying one's past losses in detail to work why they occurred. Perhaps the option concerned was too short-dated? Or did the underlying share move in the right direction but not by enough to yield a profit before expiry? Perhaps the stop-loss level was set too tight and the trade aborted too early? Or was the temptation to hang on too great and so a potentially large profit was not taken and subsequently dwindled?

All investors, even experienced ones, make mistakes like these. The important point is that, if the mistakes of the past are studied, the investor can discipline himself not to make the same mistake twice.

Choosing an Option

Dealing in the options market presents the first-time investor with a bewildering variety of choice. There are over 70 option stocks, three expiry months for each security, making a choice of over 200 classes of option. There are calls and puts on each, making a total of over 400. And finally there will be at least five exercise prices for each of the above, making upwards of 2000 possible option series to choose from. This is almost as many as the number of companies listed on the London Stock Exchange.

The investor must devise a systematic way of filtering out the right option from all those available; remembering the following points can help:

■ *Pick the Right Stock:* It sounds obvious, but selecting the right underlying stock is perhaps the most important filter of all. Later chapters explore how price charts and so-called 'technical analysis' can aid in stock selection and the timing of options purchases. But fundamental analysis also has a role to play in choosing which group of options to look at.

Fundamental analysis is about balance sheets, cash flow, profit and loss accounts, trading statements, the prospects for the industry in which the company is involved, and most important of all, management. From the standpoint of a call option buyer with over 70 option stocks to choose from, a simple filter might be to look at all those with price-earnings ratios (PERs) less than the market average and dividend yields greater than the market average.

This is not a mechanical process, however. A stock's dividend yield might be high because there is an expectation in the market that the dividend is likely to be cut. Likewise the price earnings ratio might be low because the company's earnings are expected to fall.

What to look for is consistent above average earnings growth in a stock with a PER which is at or below average. In his book *The Zulu Principle*, published by Orion Books, Jim Slater coined the term PEG (Price to Earnings Growth) Factor, to describe the relationship between a company's expected earnings growth and the price-earnings ratio on its shares. Briefly stated, for a company to be cheap, its PEG Factor has to be no more than one. In other words, if 15% earnings growth is expected on a share, it should only be bought if its price earnings ratio is less than fifteen. You need to read Jim Slater's book to understand fully this important investment yardstick.

However, growth shares do not necessarily make good option stocks. Such shares often appear expensive, but growth is rapid. The share price rises steadily. This situation may well be priced into the option, with premiums increasing steeply for longer dated calls. These situations can be played via the options market, but it may be easier to look elsewhere for a more suitable vehicle.

Where options buyers can score is by spotting turning points. This can be done through observation of price charts (as is explained in Chapter Ten), but there are other fundamental indicators to look for.

■ *Changes in outlook:* Contrary to popular belief, the market does not always react instantaneously to changes in a company's business environment. Or it may overreact, especially if the news is negative. Heavy selling of a company's shares may produce the opportunity to profit from a bounce in the share price as investors gradually realise that the news is not so bad after all.

■ *Changes at competitors:* In certain relatively homogenous sectors - brewing, food retailing, pharmaceutical, banks - developments at one company may have implications for another. These implications may well not be reflected immediately. There are opportunities here which the alert investor can exploit. A company may report good results several weeks before others in the industry. Do the share prices of all the competitors move up as a result? Do the good results mean that the company concerned has been gaining market share at the expense of the others, or are they all benefiting from common external factors, such as improved consumer spending and lower interest rates?

■ *Management changes:* These changes can be among the most potent influences over share prices. Abrupt changes in management often signify good news for the longer term outlook of a hitherto dull company. The caveat here is that the change may be followed by a period of uncertainty as some 'house-clearing' takes place, with accounting write-offs, disposals and other developments. Management changes can be internal or external ones, although in most cases new management from outside will have the most impact.

■ *Changes in directors' shareholdings:* Significant changes in directors' shareholdings can be a pointer to good news. Sales may occur for a variety of reasons relating to an individual director's personal financial circumstances, but directors buying shares, especially in significant quantities, usually means the share price is more likely than not to go up. Publications are available which review directors' dealings, and lists of these dealings are also published in an abbreviated form in the weekend edition of the *Financial Times*.

By the same token, changes in the holdings of major institutions can also be a clue as to future price trends. If a large shareholder reduces his holding, this may mean it is feeling bearish about the company's prospects, and also the reduction in the shareholding may be a prelude to further sales, which will further depress the price. Once again the market does not always react instantaneously to such news.

Because of the importance of looking at fundamentals as a way of gauging the significance or otherwise of price movements in particular stocks, and therefore whether or not they might be temporary, it is essential that would-be options investors keep a data file on each individual options company. Such a file (kept either in a computer database format, or as a physical file) might include for instance, the latest chairman's statement and salient accounts information, the nature and timing of recent announcements from the company, consensus forecasts from analysts, recent press comment about the company and the industry in which it is involved, and the likely timing of future announcements from the company - AGM, interim and final results, publication of annual report and so on.

Keeping upwards of 70 such files, given that information is released on different companies at different times of year, is not especially onerous and is good discipline and an effective way of highlighting new trading ideas. Publications are available which encapsulate some of this information, including: *The Company Guide*, published by Hemmington Scott (gives salient accounts information and contact details); *The Estimate Directory*, published by Edinburgh Financial Publishing (broker forecasts and timings of announcements); and FT McCarthy (a press cuttings service on individual companies). Some of this information is also available free of charge via the web, and many large companies now have web sites giving financial information. These are discussed in more detail in Chapter 11.

■ *Choose the right exercise price and expiry:* The timing of announcements such as company results assumes particular importance in the decision of which option and particularly which expiry date to choose. The investor may feel, for instance, that a company's results are likely to lead to a sharp upward re-rating in the shares. It is crucial to choose an option expiring after the announcement, if possible some time afterwards to allow for the necessary price adjustment to be made. One should not rely on the stockmarket discounting better prospects ahead of time.

For the first-timer, a long-dated option should theoretically offer a bigger chance that the shares will perform as expected within the life of the option and hence yield a profit. Although this will be reflected in the premium on the option, the investor can gain some comfort that he has, in relative terms, plenty of time for his judgement to be proved correct and for the underlying share's volatility to work in his favour.

Another key decision is which strike price to choose. First-time investors unused to the alarming phenomenon of time-decay are best advised to choose an option with some intrinsic value to act as a backstop against total loss. Hence a mid-expiry month deep in-the-money option, or an in-the-money option in the further expiry month may be the best choice.

For the mid-expiry month, choosing a deep in-the-money option will mean that in the event the share price does not move much, the holder will be left with significant intrinsic value on expiry and limited loss. Going back to our earlier example of Bass on page 33, imagine again it is December. The April 800 calls at $111^1/_2$p include 87p of intrinsic value and $24^1/_2$p of time value. Assuming the stock is unchanged at expiry the value of each contract will have fallen from £1,115 to £870. Buying the out-of-the-money April 900 calls at a price of $57^1/_2$p would, on the same basis, see the entire investment of £575 per contract wiped out at expiry. So, although this option costs less, the risk of total loss is much greater.

The converse of this is that gearing to any price movement in the underlying security is also greater in an out-of-the-money option. There is a way of measuring this so that the gearing element in each option can be quickly compared. This is known as the option's delta value.

The option delta measures the sensitivity of the option price to small changes in the price of the underlying share. The delta is expressed as a decimal figure between zero and one. For an at-the-money call option, the delta would normally be about 0.5. This means that for every 1p rise in the price of the underlying shares, the option price would rise 0.5p. The further in-the-money the option goes, the closer the delta gets to 1. Another way of looking at the delta value is as a measure of the probability of it being worthwhile exercising the option at expiry.

The delta is between 0 and +1 in the case of call option and 0 and -1 in the case of a put option. In this latter case this is because the price movement in the put option is in the opposite direction to the movement in the shares, the put option giving the right to sell the shares at a pre-determined price.

The delta value is calculated automatically in most standard option pricing models. These are capable of being used with ease on a normal personal computer.

The delta value shall not be viewed in isolation. One useful yardstick is to compare the delta to the price of the option. If a delta value is 0.5 for an at-the-money call priced at 10p, this is clearly more highly geared than a deep in-the-money call where the delta is 0.9 but the option price is, say, 60p.

■ *Assess Volatility:* As readers will remember from Chapter Two, one of the main components of the price of an option is the volatility of the underlying shares. The higher the volatility, the higher will be the premiums on the related options, all other things being equal. Historic option volatility is normally calculated over a comparatively short period of a matter of weeks. An option's market price may well at any time imply a level of volatility different from this historic figure. Most option pricing models calculate both implied and historic volatility.

A volatility figure can be obtained, for example, from a five-year price history and the result of this long term volatility calculation compared with the shorter term historic volatility figure, or the current level of implied volatility. Similarly, a time series of, say, three month volatility figures going back five years can be graphed and the current figures placed in this context.

How can this be used? An example might be that if a share had experienced low volatility in the recent past but had historically been much more volatile, then eventually this anomaly would be corrected. If at the same time the shares looked oversold, it would be a reasonable assumption that the correction would occur on the upside and therefore that the call options would be rewarding. Equally, higher-than-average volatility in a share which is normally more tranquil could be a prelude to a downward correction.

■ *Choose the Right Market Environment:* Equally important is to place the proposed option trade in the context of the market as a whole. A long-dated call option trade in an overbought stockmarket risks being stymied by a market correction in which all shares are automatically marked down in price by market-makers. The same goes for put option trades in oversold markets.

The flip-side of this is that buying what looks to be a cheap option in a cheap stock in an oversold market can produce a highly profitable double or triple-whammy. To profit from such strategies, however, investors need to cultivate true contrarian behaviour - to learn to resist the siren-like call of the crowd stampeding in one direction.

Such contrary thinking needs careful forward-planning and shrewd observation. First to create a game-plan to put into action if certain conditions are met, and second to observe the antics of the crowd and the symptoms of excessive speculation of an either bullish or bearish kind. The classic text on crowd psychology is Charles Mackay's book *Extraordinary Popular Delusions and the Madness of Crowds* (Harmony Books), originally published in 1841. The first 100 pages of this book deal with three famous instances of crowd madness in the sphere of financial markets. A more academic thesis on the subject is *Manias, Panics and Crashes* by Charles Kindleberger (MacMillan). Two other lighter reads on the subject of market psychology are *Panic-Proof Investing* by Tom Basso and *Investment Psychology Explained* by Martin Pring (both published by John Wiley).

It is worthwhile remembering that investors could have made substantial profits in recent years through correct option strategies at the time of the 1987 stockmarket crash (in fact some options investors lost heavily), the 1989 mini-crash, the exit of Britain from the ERM, the result of the 1992 General Election, and other events like the October 1997 worldwide market setback following the Asian currency debacle. The purpose of recommending such books is simply to alert investors to the lessons of history and the inherent characteristics of excessive boom and depression.

Summary

1. Buying options requires judgement about the direction, timing and extent of a price movement in the underlying stock.

2. A correct judgement about the likely future trend in the underlying market must also be made.

3. Options trading need not simply be speculation. Buying options is a legitimate way of establishing gearing, fixing the buying or selling price of a stock in advance, or hedging portfolio gains.

4. The advantages of purchasing options are limited and known risk, and unlimited profit potential. Their main disadvantage is the erosion in their value over time, other things being equal. Time works against the option holder and in favour of the option writer.

5. Few investors trade successfully on instinct alone. It is therefore essential, particularly for the private investor, to form a concrete action plan before the trade is initiated. This should establish a realistic expectation of how far the underlying stock may rise or fall and over what period; specify at what underlying price a profitable position will be closed; and specify what maximum level of loss will be borne. The golden rule is: if in doubt, get out.

6. Choosing the most appropriate option from the plethora available is crucial. Though charting and computer valuation models can help, it is also vital to use the fundamentals, and to be aware of the timing of significant corporate announcements.

7. The right option to buy will also be the one that provides a comfortable level of risk for the investor. For new investors this will most probably be a long-dated, deep-in-the-money call. This will have several months to run and a substantial intrinsic value which should provide a backstop against excessive loss.

8. Understanding and assessing past and potential future volatility is also important when buying options. Comparing short-term historic and implied volatility (see Chapter Two for definitions) with longer term volatility may pay dividends, especially if it is obvious the shares are overbought or unduly depressed.

FIVE

BASIC STRATEGY: BUYING CALL AND PUT OPTIONS

We have covered what options are, how they developed, how they are priced, how to select a stockbroker through whom to deal and how to establish some trading disciplines and choose the right option. The next stage is to look at options strategies. The table of key words and definitions is on page 70.

One of the advantages of equity and index options is their flexibility. They can be bought and simply held for eventual exercise. They can be sold in the market to take a profit (or loss), or (in the worst case) they can be allowed to lapse upon expiry. Options can also be combined with each other and/or with the underlying stock to provide a profit expectation appropriate to the investor's view of the outlook for the market and a particular share.

Although options deals in conjunction with the underlying stock can be executed if desired, options are commonly dealt in without the investor holding the shares. Underlying stocks and their related options can be (and are) bought and sold totally separately, through different exchanges and market-makers.

Although options will magnify the profit opportunities available to an investor if the timing and size of a price movement in the underlying security is correctly predicted, if any one of these elements is misjudged the transaction may result in a loss. Dealing costs should also be taken into account when working out profit and loss implications of particular strategies.

Alternatives Open to Investors

So options offer considerable variety to the investor. The following scenarios give a flavour of the uses to which simple options strategies can be put.

Profit from an expected share price rise - BUY CALLS

Profit from an expected share price fall - BUY PUTS

Gain exposure to a market move for minimum outlay - BUY CALLS OR PUTS

KEY TERMINOLOGY

Pay-off Diagram - a chart which shows the expected profit or loss on a particular option strategy based on different prices for the underlying share. Pay-off diagrams can either be calculated and drawn by hand, or produced through a simple computer model.

Locking-in - the use of a call (or put) option to establish a guaranteed predetermined buying (or selling) price for an underlying share. The locked-in price is the strike price of the option plus (or minus) the cost of the call (put) option.

Hedge - the purchase of options to protect a portfolio position, as a form of insurance. In the case where shares have been sold, for example, the purchase of an equivalent call means that if the shares rise in price, a corresponding rise in the option will offset the notional 'loss' in the earlier holding.

Straddle - the simultaneous purchase of a call and put in the same stock with the same expiry date and strike price. This can be used if a large movement of uncertain direction is expected in the underlying share.

Strangle - a straddle using options with different strike prices, where both the call and put options used are in-the-money.

Combination - a straddle using options with different strike prices, where both the call and put options used are out-of-the-money.

Create a geared exposure to a move in a stock or an index - BUY CALLS OR PUTS

Hedge against future uncertainty - SELL UNDERLYING STOCK AND BUY CALL or HOLD STOCK AND BUY PUT

Protect a shareholding or portfolio from a price fall - BUY PUTS

Insure against a mistimed stock purchase - BUY STOCK AND BUY PUTS

Speculate on the direction of the market - BUY INDEX CALLS OR PUTS

Protect a portfolio against an adverse market move - BUY INDEX PUTS

Strategies can also be devised which involve writing options. However, this should be done with care. The circumstances in which it can be contemplated, the risks involved and the advantages which it offers in the right circumstances are explored in the next chapter.

Option Strategies at Work

The following are some examples of how the simple strategies described above work in practice. Although we use a number of fictitious companies to illustrate the point, these strategies may apply with equal force to any of the 70 options stocks traded on LIFFE.

Example 1:

Profit from an expected share price rise - BUY CALL

VIEW: on 1st March PJT Holdings plc shares stand at 255p and a June 260 call option costs 15p. The investor expects the share price and the market to rise significantly over the following few weeks and wants to profit from the rise.

ACTION: buy one PJT June 260 call at 15p. The net outlay (ignoring dealing costs) is £150 (15p multiplied by 1,000 - the number of shares represented by each option contract). If the shares rise as expected the option can either be sold back to the market at a higher price, or the right to buy the shares can be exercised at any time up to the expiry date.

WHAT HAPPENS NEXT: the investor has correctly anticipated the rise in the share price and by 15th June (expiry day) PJT Holdings stand at 300p and the options are at 40p. The option can either be sold at a profit, or exercised and the underlying shares purchased at 260p.

PROFIT/LOSS: although both alternatives show a profit, the return on the cash invested in the options transaction is markedly different to the equivalent deal in the underlying shares. If 1,000 PJT had been bought at 255p and sold at 300p the percentage increase on an outlay of £2,550 would have been 18%. In the options market the equivalent transaction costs £150. The sale of the option prior to expiry results in the investor receiving £400 and the profit on the transaction is £250, a percentage gain of 167% on the much smaller amount invested.

SOME OTHER POSSIBLE OUTCOMES: *the shares do not move.* The option price will gradually erode as the option moves towards expiry and the time value disappears. If the investor does not move before expiry to cut his losses, the entire £150 invested will be lost.

The shares fall to 200p. If the investor does not move to cut his losses before expiry, the entire £150 invested will be lost. In the time prior to expiry the option may have some value if investors expect the share price setback to be a temporary one. In other words the time value may increase to a level above what might otherwise have been expected, because of an increase in expected volatility. Assuming the shares still stand at 200p on expiry, the option holder's loss is limited to £150. He has lost all the capital committed to the trade, but the amount involved is a comparatively small one.

If, on the other hand, the same transaction had been made in the underlying shares, the investor would have bought 1,000 shares at 255p at a cost of £2,550 and would now see them worth £2,000, a loss of £550. In percentage terms this is a smaller loss (22%) than the 100% erosion faced by the option investor, but in absolute terms the amount is larger. The holder of the underlying stock does, however, have the ability to continue to hold on in the hope that the share price will eventually recover.

CHART: the range of possible outcomes can be represented diagramatically as shown in *Chart 1* on page 73. This shows the position at expiry, when the value of the option consists simply of its intrinsic value, if any. Charts like this are sometimes known as pay-off diagrams and should always be consulted before embarking on an option transaction. They can either be drawn by hand by calculating the profit/loss outcome at different levels of the underlying price, or arrived at on a simple computer model as described in Chapter Eight.

The break even point for the options investor is the point at which the profit line crosses the horizontal axis and occurs at, in this instance, 275p. This is the 260p strike price plus the 15p cost of the option. Once the share price rises above 275p, the option holder can sell at a profit, while the maximum loss under any circumstances is limited to the 15p cost of the option, represented in the chart by the horizontal line below the horizontal axis.

Although this chart represents the position on expiry day, the option holder is free to sell his option at any time prior to expiry and, if so, would receive the intrinsic value of the option (the share price less the strike price) plus any remaining time value.

PJT Holdings Option Strategy
Buy 1 June 260 Call @ 15p

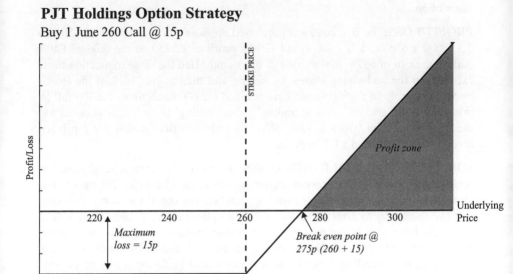

Chart 1: PJT Holdings - profiting from an expected price rise.

Example 2:

Profit from an expected share price fall – BUY PUT

VIEW: it is 1st March and you believe that not only is the market too high but that Beresford Breweries' results, due in the next few weeks, will be disappointing and that the price will therefore fall sharply from its present level of 270p.

ACTION: buy five June 260 puts at 8p. The total cost is £400 excluding dealing costs (5 x 1,000 x 8p). If the shares fall sharply as expected, the options can be sold back to the market before expiry at a profit. Exercise is only possible if you hold the shares, although the shares could be bought at the lower market price immediately prior to exercise for this purpose and then effectively sold - via exercising the put - at the higher strike price.

WHAT HAPPENS NEXT: the results are announced on 1st April, and are worse than expected. The share price immediately falls to 200p. The option has lost some time value in the meantime but is now priced at 63p. This is comprised of intrinsic value of 60p (ie. the amount the share price is below the strike price) and time value of 3p.

PROFIT/LOSS: the five contracts purchased are now worth a total of £3,150 (ie. 5 x 1,000 x 63p) and, if sold, would yield a profit of £2,750 on the original £400 outlay, a return of 687% in the space of one month. Had the same transaction been executed in the underlying shares, by selling and then buying back at the lower price, a net profit of £3,500 would have resulted (5,000 shares times the 70p fall in price). With the end of 'account trading', 'short selling' is no longer possible for the private investor. Options now offer the only practical means for a private investor to benefit from a fall in price.

SOME OTHER POSSIBLE OUTCOMES: *the shares do not move at all from the original price of 270p.* The option expires worthless on 15th June. The time value element in the option will erode as expiry approaches. The option investor loses £400.

The shares rise to 320p rather than fall. The options expire worthless and, unless they have been sold in the meantime, the option investor loses the entire option premium paid of £400. In this eventuality if the equivalent transaction had been possible in the underlying shares, the investor would be facing a loss of £2,500, having sold 5,000 shares at 270p and being forced to look at buying them back at 320p to cover his liability. The share investor might hold on in the hope that the rise was a temporary one, but would face the risk of the price moving even further against him.

CHART: The range of possibilities can be seen in *Chart 2* on page 75 showing the profit profile of the put option at expiry.

As can be seen, this chart is the mirror image of *Chart 1* on page 73 for the equivalent call option, with the profit increasing the lower the level of the underlying share price. In this case the break even point for the option investor is again the point at which the sloping line crosses the horizontal axis – at 252p – (the strike price of the option - 260p - minus the 8p cost of buying it). Part of the 8p cost of the option (which in this instance represents just time value) may be recouped if the option is sold prior to expiry.

The profit potential in the put option is not unlimited, unlike the call. The maximum profit possible would be 252p per share – made if the underlying share price fell to zero, an unlikely event.

These two examples demonstrate not only the gearing effect of options in the sense of the percentage return gained for a lower outlay, but also the slightly different characteristics of calls and puts when compared to the underlying transactions against which they could be measured.

Beresford Breweries Option Strategy

Buy 1 June 260 Put @ 8p

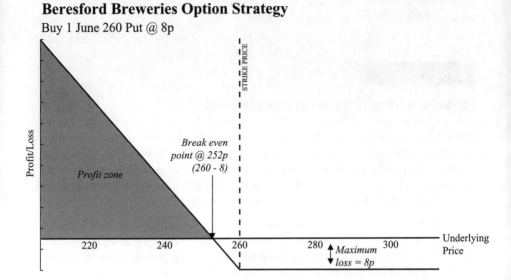

Chart 2: Beresford Breweries - profiting from an expected share price fall.

It can probably also be seen instinctively from the examples that options can be used as a way of establishing a target price for buying or selling an underlying share.

By using options a particular price can be 'locked in' for the duration of the option if a shortage of funds, or worries about the underlying level of the stockmarket, make it inappropriate to deal immediately in the underlying shares. In the case of a buying decision, the locked-in price is equivalent to the strike price of the call option plus its cost. In the case of a decision to sell, the locked-in selling price is the cost of the put option subtracted from its strike price.

In Example 1 on page 71, therefore, if the transaction is looked at as a way of locking-in a price for a future purchase, the locked-in price is 275p.

Although this is 20p more than the present price, the investor's only outlay for the moment is the cost of the option. Compared to buying the stock outright, the difference between this outlay and the total cost of buying the shares at 275p is available for deployment elsewhere, possibly in some form of interest-bearing account, for the remaining three months of the option's life.

In conjunction with a holding in the underlying stock, options might be used either to protect an existing shareholding from a temporary price drop, or so as not to miss out from a further rise in the share price if a holding has been sold. These are dealt with in the following examples.

Example 3:

Protect a holding from an expected fall - BUY PUT

VIEW: it is 1st March. The investor holds 5,000 Software Investments plc shares currently worth 270p a share. The shares were previously purchased some time ago at 180p. The results, due in a few weeks time, may be worse than the stockmarket expects and a price fall is anticipated. However, the investor believes that the price may recover and does not therefore want to disturb the holding.

ACTION: buy 5 Software Investments June 260 puts at 8p. The 5,000 shares represented by the five contracts match exactly the underlying holding and the investor will be protected against a price fall below 252p. In other words, he will secure a guaranteed minimum selling price of 252p (ie. the strike price of 260p minus the 8p cost of the option).

WHAT HAPPENS NEXT: as expected, a month later the results are announced, and are viewed as disappointing. The shares fall back to 200p. The put option is now priced at 66p having lost a little time value in the meantime, an erosion more than made good by the fact that it now has substantial intrinsic value.

PROFIT/LOSS: in this instance the value of the original holding of 5,000 shares has declined from 270p to 200p, or by £3,500. The put options purchased have, however, increased in price from 8p to 66p giving a profit per share of 58p, or a total profit of 5,000 x 58p - £2,900. As a result of the transaction the loss which would have occurred has been reduced from £3,500 to just £600, once the offsetting profit in the puts is taken into account. An insurance premium of £400 (the cost of the options) has limited the loss in the value to £600, thereby saving £2,900.

SOME OTHER POSSIBLE OUTCOMES: *the price remains unchanged.* The options expire worthless and the investor loses the £400 cost of the options. The value of the holding, and any profit already accrued on it, remain intact but for the cost of the 'insurance'.

The results are disappointing but, on the same day they are announced, the company receives a takeover bid at 380p. The options are sold to recoup the remaining time value. The time value has decreased sharply because of the change in perceived volatility as a result of the takeover bid and is now only 2p. The net loss on the options is thus 6p per share or £300 for the five contracts. However, the value of the shares has risen to 380p from their original purchase price of 180p, increasing the total profit on the holding to £10,000 - an increase of £5,500 over the position a month previously. The option holder may rue the loss of the option premium, but only the most avaricious would worry about this in the context of the substantial additional profit which has accrued on the underlying holding.

The investor may, however, now take the view that he wishes to lock in the profit in the event that, say, the bid is referred to the Monopolies Commission, while continuing to hold the shares in case a higher offer is received for the company. A different put option series can thus be purchased to do this from the higher price base.

CHART: *Chart 3* below demonstrates the net position **at expiry** that the investor enjoys as a result of hedging the position using the put option. Note that the shape of the chart is similar to that of a straightforward call option purchase, as shown in the example on page 73. In other words, a purchase of a call has the equivalent risk profile to holding the shares but buying puts as a 'hedge'.

Software Investments Option Strategy
• Hold 1000 shares @ 270p Buy 1 June 260 Put @ 8p – 'Hedge'

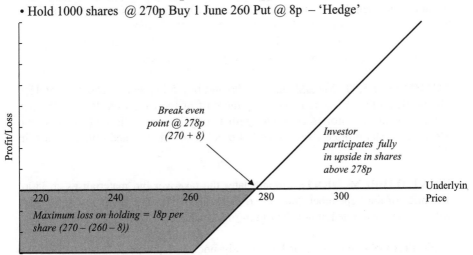

Chart 3: Software Investments - protecting a holding against a share price fall.

The chart also demonstrates the important aspect of buying a put as a way of insuring against a mistimed stock purchase. In this instance an equivalent number of puts are bought to hedge the purchase (ie. one contract per 1,000 shares purchased). In the example above, if the shares were bought at 270p and the 260 put purchased at the same time for 8p, the holder of the stock would participate fully in any rise in the shares beyond the 270p purchase price plus the cost of the option (ie. 278p), but be protected against any price fall below 260p. An alternative way of looking at this is that the investor derives the full profit from any rise in price, but has insurance below the 252p level (the strike price of the option minus its cost).

The reverse use of this technique is to protect against having sold too soon if a share continues to rise. This can be achieved by selling the shares but at the same time buying an equivalent number of calls to hedge the transaction. This is shown in the example below:

Example 4:

Insure against a mistimed share sale - BUY CALL

VIEW: it is now 1st July. An investor holds 5,000 MegaMedia plc shares purchased at 180p. The MegaMedia share price is now 270p. The investor is nervous about the future outlook for the stockmarket and the fact that a rumoured takeover hasn't yet materialised and decides to take his profit. He wants, however, to insure against missing out on a greater profit if the price appreciates further.

ACTION: sell 5,000 MegaMedia at 270p and buy 5 September 280 calls at 15p. The profit on the shares is reduced by the cost of the calls from 90p to 75p per share, but the investor is covered against forgoing an additional profit if the MegaMedia share price rises above 280p between 1st July and option expiry in September.

WHAT HAPPENS NEXT: a month later the takeover bid materialises at 380p. The price of the September 280 calls rises to 110p. The option has lost some time value in the meantime but now has an intrinsic value of 100p.

PROFIT/LOSS: the investor has already pocketed the profit from selling the original holding at 270p. This profit was 75p per share after allowing for the cost of the option 'insurance'. The total gain on this original transaction was therefore

£3,750. The five call option contracts purchased at the time the sale was concluded can now be sold for 110p, yielding £5,500 or a profit of £4,750. The total gain is £8,500. If the shares had simply been held throughout, the gain on the shares originally purchased at 180p would have been £10,000, £1,500 more than the gain as a result of the sale and call purchase transaction. Once again, the investor protects himself against the risk of an adverse outcome (in this case a notional profit foregone) by giving up part of the realised gain.

SOME OTHER POSSIBLE OUTCOMES: *the share price stays at more or less the same level and the option eventually expires worthless.* This is probably the worst outcome of all. In this instance the investor loses the cash committed to the option transaction, unless he sells prior to expiry to recoup some of the time value. The effect is the same as a sale at below the market price to no purpose.

The share price declines to 200p. The investor has in effect sold the shares at 255p (the price of 270p less the cost of the option) but the option has again served no purpose and, in hindsight, the straight sale would have proved the better course of action.

The profit/loss profile of this course of action is shown in the *Chart 4* below. As before, this represents the position at expiry of the option.

MegaMedia Option Strategy
• Sell 1000 shares @ 270 • Buy 1 September 280 Call @ 15p – 'Hedged Sale'

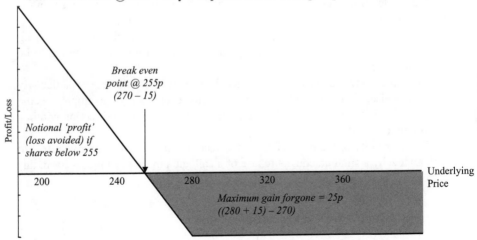

Chart 4: MegaMedia - insuring against a mistimed share sale.

Using options in this way is like any form of insurance. The greater the amount of cover required, the higher will be the cost. In the cases outlined above, the insurance purchased is in the form of a medium-dated slightly out-of-the-money option. For most purposes, and unless the hedging activity is geared to a specific event which is expected to occur within either a few days or not for several months, this probably represents the optimum risk-reward ratio. The option is long-dated enough for erosion of time value not to be particularly marked, while the out-of-the-money nature of the option means the insurance is relatively cheap. However the hedge is not a perfect one, since the risk is not completely offset.

In-the-money options would provide a more complete level of insurance cover, but at a higher cost. However, the profit/loss profile can be fine-tuned, if need be, by over-hedging slightly. In the examples above, although the transaction in the underlying shares was in 5,000 shares, buying six, rather than five, options contracts would produce a greater level of insurance at comparatively low cost. In Example 3, for instance, buying six contracts instead of five would produce an extra £580 of profit at the cost of £80 for the additional contract, a net gain of £500 sharply reducing the overall loss on the transaction.

Straddles

The four examples above show the most common uses of options by the private investor. These are, in short, the use of options as a way of gearing up one's exposure to an expected price movement, the locking-in of a purchase or sale price, and the use of options as a way of hedging against an unexpected movement in the price of underlying shares which have been recently purchased or sold.

The common feature of all these strategies, however, is that the underlying price movement required to make the option transaction a profitable one has to be in a defined direction.

There may, however, be occasions when the market is directionless or particularly volatile, or else when uncertainty over an external event (a good example was the 1992 General Election) could make prices move sharply in either direction within a specific time period.

The flexibility of the options market is such that it is possible to give effect to such a view by a simultaneous purchase of a call and put. In its simplest form, this strategy is known, for obvious reasons, as a straddle.

Example 5:

Capturing a big move in either direction - A STRADDLE

VIEW: it is 1st March. In a month's time the outcome of a Government investigation into the nuclear power industry will be announced. Fusion Thermonuclear's price has been affected by the uncertainty involved in the investigation. If the industry is given a clean bill of health, the share price should rise. If not, continuing uncertainty will depress the price further. The investor wishes to take advantage of a possible sharp move in either direction in the shares from their present level of 270p.

ACTION: buy one Fusion Thermonuclear June 260 call at 25p and buy one June 260 put at 7p. This establishes a profit zone if the share price moves outside 292p on the upside and 228p on the downside. This is because the total cost of the two options (32p) is borne irrespective of the direction of the eventual move. The strategy requires an 8% move on the upside to break even and a 16% move on the downside. The strike price of the option chosen may therefore be tailored to bias the break even point in the direction viewed as more likely. If either outcome were considered equally likely, then the strike price nearest the current share price would be chosen.

WHAT HAPPENS NEXT: on 1st April the Government announces that the investigation into the industry is to continue and that it is considering legislation to curb its monopoly power. Fusion's price drops on this news to 190p. The time value of the puts has dropped in the meantime to 5p, but they now also have an intrinsic value of 70p and a total value of 75p. The 260 calls now have no intrinsic value but a time value of 3p. The chances of the price recovering before the option expires is remote, but not impossible. However, since the direction of the move has become clear and there is a profit on the put side of the straddle the call side can be closed immediately to defray part of the original cost of the strategy.

PROFIT/LOSS: the put can be sold to raise £750. The sale of the call side raises £30, making a total of £780. The total cost of the strategy was £320 (1,000 x 25p plus 1,000 x 7p). The overall profit is therefore £460 on an original outlay of £320, a gain of 144%.

SOME OTHER POSSIBLE OUTCOMES: *the announcement is as before but the shares only move down to 240p.* The calls have a time value of 5p because of the slightly higher probability of a bounce-back in the share price. But the intrinsic value of the puts of 20p plus their remaining time value of 5p means that the overall position can be closed at a small loss. The aggregate value of the call and put

(30p: ie. 5p for the calls, plus a total value of 25p for the puts) is less than the 32p net cost of the strategy.

Since the options still have some time to run and the combined time value is small relative to the intrinsic value of the put, it may be worth continuing to hold the put in the hope that the shares slip further once the announcement has been fully digested. The call side of the strategy can probably be closed to reduce the time value element in the strategy, which then becomes a straight put.

The Government announces that it needs another six months to complete the investigation into the industry and the shares continue to languish around the 270p mark. Time passes and both options expire worthless leaving the investor with a total loss of £320 on 15th June, unless the position is closed beforehand to recoup the remaining time value in the options. In practice this would probably be done immediately the announcement of the delay took place. In these circumstances, the time value of the options would probably also fall immediately due to a reduction in the expected volatility of the shares.

The profit/loss chart of this strategy at expiry is shown in *Chart 5* below.

Fusion Thermonuclear Option Strategy
• Buy 1 June 260 Call @ 25p • Buy 1 June 260 Put @ 7p – 'Straddle'

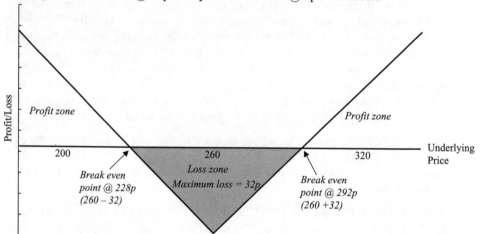

Chart 5: Fusion Thermonuclear - a Straddle strategy.

This can be viewed as essentially the combination of a call chart and a put chart as shown on page 82, with the difference that the 'loss zone' - which reflects the fact that the cost of buying two options has to be borne - is somewhat larger than for each of the options individually.

Strangles and Combinations

The example above represents a classic straddle, where both call and put have the same strike price. It can be seen, however, that for the assumption of the equal probability of an upside and downside move to be given effect, this strategy has some drawbacks. The degree to which the trade will benefit from an upward or downward move depends on the relationship of the strike price to the underlying share price. In the example above, although the strike price is the same for both the call and the put, the call is in-the-money but the put is therefore, by definition, out-of-the-money.

There is no need for the call and put side of the strategy to have the same strike price provided the expiry date is the same. A straddle can therefore be constructed whereby both options are in-the-money, or both out-of-the-money. A straddle where both options are in-the-money is known as a strangle. Where both options are out-of-the-money, the strategy is known as a combination.

The obvious advantage of a strangle is that, although each option will cost more and therefore the break even point be extended, if the expected move in the price either up or down does not take place, the transaction will have some residual intrinsic value on expiry. The extent of the loss incurred will be to some degree limited.

Say for the sake of argument that the price of Wunderkind Industries plc is around the 247p mark. It is now 1st August. The price of the October 240 calls is 20p and the 260 puts are 18p. A strangle can be established for a net cost of 38p. The break even point on the call side of the strategy is 278p (240p plus 38p) and on the put side 222p (260p minus 38p). As in the straddle the upside potential outside of either of these break even points is unlimited, while the loss is limited to the net cost of the strategy less the combined intrinsic value. In the case of the call the intrinsic value is 7p and in the case of the put it is 13p. The maximum loss on the strategy is therefore 18p. *Chart 6* on page 84 illustrates this.

In this case it can be seen that the shape of the chart is broadly similar to the straddle but the chart's profile has been 'flattened'. The break even points are wider apart, but the loss zone is smaller in area, without the 'v' at the bottom of the chart.

If both options are out-of-the-money the chart looks broadly similar, but the cost of the combination strategy is less because of the lack of any intrinsic value in either option. All three strategies (straddle, strangle and combination) are appropriate

Wunderkind Industries Option Strategy
• Buy 1 October 240 Call @ 20p • Buy 1 October 260 Put @ 18p – 'Strangle'

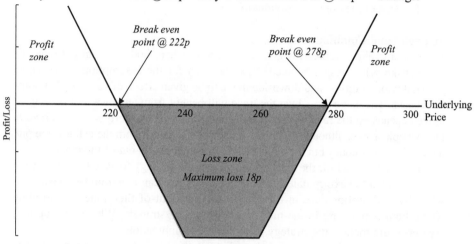

Chart 6: Wunderkind Industries - Strangle strategy.

if the investor thinks that volatility in a particular share is likely, but is unsure about the direction it will take.

The strangle is the most conservative strategy of the three because the buyer has some intrinsic value to fall back on. Likewise the combination which is shown in *Chart 7* on page 85, is the most risky since the buyer can lose the entire cost of the strategy if the expected move does not take place. In both cases the break even points are extended and, as in any option purchase strategy, the passage of time works against the holder.

Wunderkind Industries Option Strategy

• Buy 1 October 260 Call @ 10p • Buy 1 October 240 Put @ 15p – 'Combination'

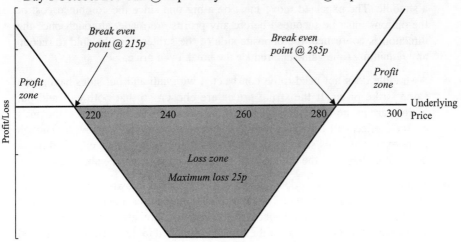

Chart 7: Wunderkind Industries - Combination strategy.

Summary

1. Most option transactions by private investors consist of buying calls or puts. The advantage of buying options is that the upside potential is unlimited, and the loss is limited to the cost of the option. The disadvantage is that time works against the holder, with the option's time value eroding as expiry approaches.

2. Options can be bought and traded without the investor necessarily holding the underlying share. They can be bought to gain gearing and exposure to an anticipated move in the market or the shares of a particular company, and to establish a maximum buying or minimum selling price in advance.

3. Options can also be used to insure against (hedge) a possible incorrect buying or selling decision in the underlying shares. A purchase can be hedged (against the possibility of the shares subsequently going down) by simultaneously buying a put. A sale can be hedged (against a further subsequent rise in the shares) by buying a call at the same time as the holding is sold.

4. Options can be used to speculate on a sharp movement in a share price irrespective of its direction. This can be done by simultaneously buying a call and put with the same exercise price and expiry date. This strategy is known as a straddle. The expected move must be a big one since the combined cost of the options must be recouped before any profits are made, although once the direction is confirmed, the opposite side of the strategy can be sold to recoup any remaining time value and reduce the break even price.

5. A straddle does not need to be constructed with call and put sides having the same strike price. If the strike prices are chosen so that both call and put options are in-the-money, this is known as a strangle. In this instance, the put's exercise price will be above the share price, and the call's below it. Though more expensive, this strategy is more conservative since if the expected move does not materialise, the options will still have some intrinsic value at expiry.

6. A straddle where both options are out-of-the-money is known as a combination. Here the strategy is cheaper, but the expected move to achieve break even will be greater, and the investor, because the options purchased possess only time value, faces the total erosion of the capital committed to the trade if the expected move does not take place before expiry.

SIX

BASIC STRATEGY: WRITING OPTIONS

The table of key words and definitions is on page 88. Many articles and textbooks on options caution readers on writing (selling) options, since this can open up the possibility of unlimited loss. If so, why do it at all?

The circumstance in which unlimited risk is involved is known as uncovered, or 'naked', writing. It involves the investor selling a call (or put) option when he or she does not have the underlying stock (or cash) to satisfy the holder of the option in the event of exercise. But writing options can be used in combination with other options trades and with underlying stock purchases and sales. In these instances, the risk involved is limited.

The private investor should never contemplate naked option writing. It is also essential when writing options under other circumstances always to be aware of the risk profile being assumed as a result.

Why Write Options?
With this warning in mind, why write options at all? To recap from earlier chapters, an option writer is an investor whose initial or opening transaction is an option sale. The writer receives the option premium from the buyer. This is retained by the writer under all circumstances. In exchange the writer assumes the obligation to make (or take, in the case of a put) delivery of the stock in the event the option buyer wishes to exercise this right at any time during the option's life.

Since exercise can involve the writer in a substantial financial commitment, LIFFE - through the London Clearing House (LCH) - requires that a writer deposits and at all times maintains sufficient funds with the broker or LIFFE member through whom the deal is executed to ensure that the obligations of the contract can be met in full. These funds are known as margin. The margin required for a particular transaction is calculated by means of a complex computer program which assesses amongst other things the volatility of a particular security and the resulting probability of the writer being called upon to fulfil his obligations as a result of exercise.

KEY TERMINOLOGY

Uncovered (or 'Naked') Writing - writing an option without having the stock (or cash) to cover the obligations of the call (or put) option in the event that it is exercised by the option holder. Uncovered writing leaves the writer open to the risk of unlimited loss and should be avoided by the private investor under all circumstances.

Covered Writing - writing an option in conjunction with a holding in the underlying shares equivalent to, or greater than, that implied by the option or (in the case of a put), sufficient cash to purchase the underlying shares at the exercise price.

Buy-write Strategy - writing a call option in conjunction with a simultaneous purchase of the equivalent amount of underlying shares.

Static Return - the return received from a covered-write strategy if the underlying shares remain broadly unchanged, comprising dividend income (if any) and the option premium.

'If Called' Return - the return received from a covered-write strategy if the shares move by sufficient to trigger exercise of the written option, comprising dividend income (if any), the premium on the option and the gain in the underlying price up to the exercise level.

The bulk of the writer's margin will be deposited at the time the transaction is initiated. This is known as **initial margin**. But margin can vary from day to day. If the market or the individual stock concerned enters a period of greater volatility the investor may face calls from his broker for additional margin payments, known as **variation margin**. If volatility drops, the writer may get a margin refund.

Acceptable forms of margin are various forms of cash, near-cash and securities. In the case of an equity option, margin may take the form of a holding in the underlying shares. In practice the broker would normally ask the investor for a greater amount of margin than would theoretically be required for writing a particular option, in order to avoid the need for any later calls for smaller amounts of additional margin which could become necessary, very often to the extent of being fully covered.

It is essential for the investor to understand fully at the outset the amount of margin required, the acceptable forms of margin, and the requirement for making additional margin deposits as and when necessary.

In the earlier chapters about buying options, we described the way in which an option holder faces the erosion in time value of the option. Time works against the option holder.

For the writer, the opposite is true. The passage of time makes it progressively less likely that the option will be capable of being exercised profitably.

Despite a general perception that the market is becoming more volatile, the big moves required to generate a useful profit on the purchase of an option, either a call or a put, are rarer than they might seem. For the duration of a particular option, it is likely, more often than not, that the price will move by less than is needed to yield a profit for the purchaser.

Writing options, with appropriate safeguards and in the full awareness of the risks involved, is therefore an appropriate strategy for those whose view on the market, or on a particular stock, is neutral to slightly bullish or bearish.

Those with a neutral to slightly bearish view should write a call option; those with a neutral to slightly bullish view should write a put option. It is also worth remembering that option prices are higher the greater the perceived volatility of a particular share. If, in formulating a view about the suitability or otherwise of a particular trade, the investor believes that a particular share has been unduly volatile in the recent past (a fact reflected in high premiums for options on that particular stock) but is likely to 'quieten down' significantly over the following few weeks and months, then writing an option may be an appropriate strategy.

Simple Option Writing
The examples below demonstrate the mathematics of option writing. They are intended to demonstrate the risks of uncovered option writing and should serve as a warning to investors contemplating such action.

Example 6:

Writing a CALL

VIEW: you, the investor, believe that the defence contractor Chopper Helicopters plc, whose price has been unusually volatile ahead of its annual results, will quieten down now that the announcement has been made. The price is unlikely to move much from its present level for the next few months. It is currently 1st July, and the shares are trading at 255p.

ACTION: you write ten September 260 calls at a price of 15p. You receive £1,500 but are exposed to the movement in 10,000 of the underlying shares for almost three months, until the September series expires on 28th September. You will suffer no loss unless the shares move above 275p (ie. 260p + 15p) in the intervening period.

WHAT HAPPENS NEXT: your judgement has proved incorrect. Chopper announces that it has won a substantial contract to supply helicopters to the Ministry of Defence for the next five years, an order which will result in its factories being able to work at full capacity for the whole of that period. The company forecasts a substantial uplift in profits in the year which has just begun. The shares immediately rise to 375p and the options are exercised against you.

PROFIT/LOSS: because you were a naked writer you do not have the stock to deliver to the option holder and must therefore go into the market to buy it. You buy 10,000 shares at 375p at a cost of £37,500 and are exercised against to immediately deliver the shares to the option holder: you receive the exercise price of 260p in return, a total of £26,000. The loss of £11,500 is offset by the £1,500 option premium which you, as the writer, still keep, but your overall net loss is still £10,000. You have lost more than six times the amount you received for writing the option, despite the fact that the shares have only moved 47% from their price at the time you first wrote the option.

SOME OTHER POSSIBLE OUTCOMES: *the company announces the winning of the Government order, but the market has already anticipated it.* The shares move up to 260p on confirmation of the news. At this price it is not worth option holders exercising their options. The options eventually expire worthless and you keep the option premium.

Despite rumours in the market about a Government contract, no announcement is made, and the shares drop back to 230p. The 260 calls are now 30p out-of-the-money and increasingly unlikely to be exercised. You can either close the trade in the market by buying back the options at a lower price or else leave them to expire worthless, trusting that nothing will happen in the meantime to cause the price to rise sharply.

CHART: *Chart 8* on page 91 shows the profile of a call option at expiry from the standpoint of the writer. The maximum profit is shown by the horizontal line and the increasing loss by the diagonal line which dips below the horizontal axis and into a loss-making position if the share price moves above the break even point of 275p.

Chopper Helicopters Option Strategy

Write 1 September 260 call @ 15p

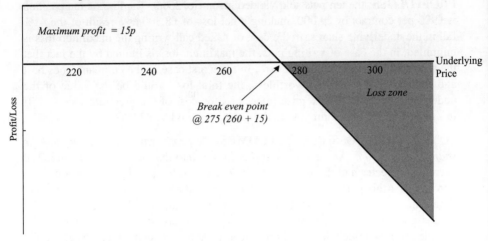

Chart 8: Chopper Helicopters plc – risks of 'naked' call writing.

Example 7:

Writing a PUT

VIEW: you believe that Eurobank plc, whose shares had been particularly volatile ahead of their recent results, will now quieten down. Since the price is unlikely to move much, or may simply drift up a little in line with the market, you decide to write a put. Again the underlying price on 1st July is 255p.

ACTION: write ten September 240 puts at a price per share of 7p. Because the put is out-of-the-money the entire premium is time value. The income from writing the put is £700 and the position will be profitable unless the price of the shares falls below 233p, (ie. 240p – 7p) a 9% drop from the present level.

WHAT HAPPENS NEXT: the shares move little until three weeks before expiry, when the company issues a profit warning. The shares drop to 150p and the put option is exercised. You are obliged to buy the shares from the option holder at

91

240p (90p above the current market price). You do not have the full amount of cash to fund this purchase and so must sell the shares immediately and realise a loss.

PROFIT/LOSS: the ten puts sold yielded income of £700. The loss on the position is £900 per contract or £9,000, making a net loss of £8,300 as a result of the 41% fall in the underlying shares. In the case of naked call writing the maximum loss is unlimited; in the case of writing puts, the maximum loss is limited by the fact that the share price cannot fall below zero. In the worst case, if the company goes bust and the shares are deemed worthless, the total loss would be the value of the underlying shares at the exercise price, less the cost of the premium received. If this happened the maximum loss in the example would be £23,300.

SOME OTHER POSSIBLE OUTCOMES: *the profit warning is issued and the shares fall to 230p.* As the option moves further into the money, the likelihood of exercise is greater and the writer may choose to cut his loss by making a closing purchase. At this point, three weeks from expiry, the options have lost significant time value and are priced at 13p (10p intrinsic value and 3p time value). The purchase of ten contracts costs £1,300, leaving the investor with a loss of £600. This decision is a finely balanced one because exercise may not take place, and the writer may be closing the position needlessly. For example, an option with a small amount of intrinsic value may not be exercised because the transaction costs involved may outweigh any profit.

The shares react little to the profit warning. They are marked down as low as 220p but immediately bounce. No option exercise takes place as option holders are banking, incorrectly as it turns out, on the shares eventually falling further. The option writer keeps the premium.

CHART: *Chart 9* on page 93 shows the profile of the written (or short) put option position at expiry. The potential loss increases the lower shares go below the break even point of 233p.

Covered Writing
The more normal (and safer) use of call option writing is when it is done in conjunction with a position in the underlying stock. This is known as covered writing and differs from naked writing to the extent that the writer will - in the worst case that the option is exercised against him - be able to supply the necessary stock from his holding. This has a known cost. The writer avoids having to go into the market and buy stock at a higher price than the exercise price and take an instant loss.

The covered writer of a put is one with sufficient funds available to cover the

Eurobank Option Strategy

Write 1 September 240 put @ 7p

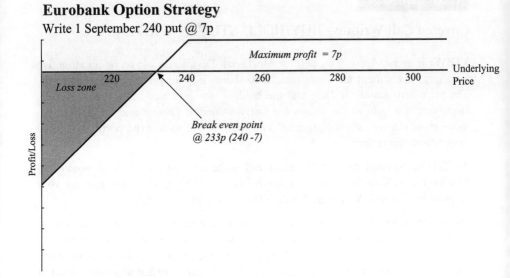

Chart 9: Eurobank plc – risks of 'naked' put writing.

position if exercise takes place, without being a forced seller of the stock of which he is obliged to take delivery.

Call writing is normally undertaken against an existing holding (which may have been held for some time). The view may be taken that the price is unlikely to move substantially over the life of the option. The holder wishes to use the option market to gain additional portfolio income. The income derives from the premium received on writing the call.

The alternative strategy, known as a 'buy-write' strategy, occurs when a stock purchase is made, perhaps as a long term investment, and a call with a higher exercise price is immediately written. The premium from writing the call effectively goes towards reducing the cost of the purchase of the underlying stock, and also establishes a maximum profit potential (equivalent to the exercise price of the call plus the premium received) beyond which any further gains in the stock will be foregone for the life of the option. If the share price moves beyond this level the option will be exercised by the holder and the writer will have the underlying stock called away.

Example 8:

Covered Call Writing - BUY/HOLD STOCK - WRITE CALL

VIEW: it is 1st April. You believe Mactavish Distilleries plc to be an attractive long term investment and have had 5,000 shares in your portfolio for some time. The price now stands at 288p and the holding was purchased at a price of 200p. However, you believe the shares are fairly valued at present and are unlikely to move significantly for a few months. You wish to gain some extra portfolio income or downside protection.

ACTION: continue to hold the stock but write calls against it. You would feel comfortable selling the stock if it appreciated to 315p, a 58% plus gain on your original investment. You write 5 July 300 calls at a price of 15p.

PROFIT/LOSS: this action yields £750 of additional portfolio income on top of your original profit £4,400. Alternatively, your profit in the stock is protected unless the stock drops below 273p, the current price less the 15p premium received. The option will be exercised against you and your holding called away if the shares rise above 300p but the extra income gained from writing the options means your effective sale price will be 315p. Alternatively if the shares stay below 300p for the life of the option, but above 273p, you will have had the best of both worlds.

The maximum profit potential is achieved at, say, 299p on expiry. That is to say the stock has gone up by fractionally less than is required to make it worthwhile the option holder exercising. At this point the writer has had a further 11p of appreciation in the underlying stock plus the 15p per share premium for writing the call.

SOME OTHER POSSIBLE OUTCOMES: if at this point it looks as though the shares may rise through the exercise price the position can be closed (ie. the equivalent call option bought) taking advantage of the erosion of the premium for whatever time has elapsed and maintaining the exposure to the upward movement in the shares through the underlying holding.

For instance, on 20th July the shares, which have been static since the beginning of April begin to start moving up towards the 300p mark. It is important to note that the stock may well not be automatically called away immediately the shares breach the 300p mark. Option holders who have bought the options at 15p will not yet be fully breaking even. Rather than undergo the expense of exercising and buying the underlying stock, they may gamble that the upsurge will continue and be reflected quickly in the price of the options, even though expiry is close.

At 305p, with expiry a week away, the July 300 calls are priced at 6p. At this point, closing the option position through buying the calls yields a net gain on the option position of 9p (sold/written at 15p, bought back at 6p) on five contracts - a net gain of £450, whilst the investor (who still holds the underlying stock) now has undiluted exposure to any further upside in the price.

Even in the event that the option position must be closed at a loss (if for instance the upward move in the underlying stock occurs soon after the trade is initiated) this need not be the end of the story. A further alternative open to the investor is to write a longer-dated call with a higher exercise price. This may well produce a higher premium than the loss being taken on the initial transaction, and leaves the investor with a new target price below which he will participate in any appreciation in the share price. This strategy is known as 'walking up' the position.

CHART: the following chart shows the net position on expiry which results from the long position in the stock and the written calls. The net break even point is shifted to the left as a result of the premium on the written call, but the potential gain is capped for any rise in the stock above the 315p mark.

Mactavish Distilleries Option Strategy

Write 1 July 300 call @ 15p against existing holding of 1000 shares @ 288p
– Covered Write

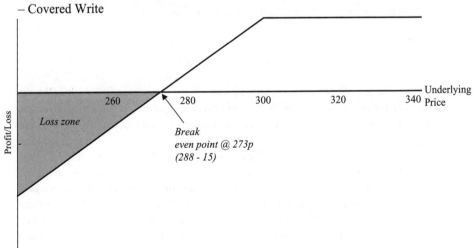

Chart 10: Mactavish Distilleries plc – covered call writing.

Covered writing and 'buy-write' strategies, essentially similar in concept, clearly involve a trade off between the amount of downside protection (or additional portfolio income) offered in exchange for forgoing upside participation in the price beyond a certain level.

The balance between these two factors can be adjusted by varying the degree to which the written option is in or out-of-the-money. The deeper in-the-money, the greater the downside protection, since the premium will be higher, but the greater the chance of exercise. This is because the option, having significant intrinsic value initially, is more likely to be exercised. The deeper out-of-the-money, the lower the level of income and downside protection gained, but the greater the degree of upside participation before the stock is called away.

Arguably it makes little sense to write a deep in-the-money call except perhaps as part of a more complex strategy, since the risk that the position will be disturbed by a holder exercising is that much greater. The ideal use of a covered call strategy might well be to write the call so as to necessitate at least a 10% upward move in the underlying stock before the point is reached where exercise becomes likely.

This brings one to the question of measuring the returns derived from writing call options.

Static and 'If Called' Returns

The benefit derived from covered call writing can be measured in terms of a rate of return calculation which covers the two main outcomes the writer is likely to face: either the option is not exercised, or it is. The investor makes a return in both cases. These are known, respectively, as the static return and the 'if called' return.

The static return measures the return to the investor if the price of the underlying shares remains static. The amount received by the investor amounts to the option premium plus any dividends paid on the underlying shares during the life of the option. The amount invested, the denominator of the equation, is the capital invested in the holding of underlying shares less the amount of option premium received for writing the option.

Calculating the static return can be demonstrated by a simple example.

Assume a 260 call option with three months to run. The underlying shares are 240p and the option is priced at 10p. Establishing a covered write entails buying the shares at 240p and selling the option for 10p. The amount invested (the bottom half of the equation) is therefore 230p (240p outlay less 10p option premium received). The return (the top half of the equation) is 10p. But imagine also that a dividend of 2p is paid during the life of the option.

The static return is therefore:

$$\frac{10+2}{240-10} = 5.2\%$$

However, this return is earned over the space of three months of the year. The same return could in theory be earned four times in the space of a year. On an annualised basis, therefore, it is 20.8% (5.2% x 4). For less neat periods to expiry the annualisation factor is a multiplier calculated by dividing 365 (days in a year) by the number of days to expiry at the time the option is written.

Assume now that before expiry the price of the shares rose to 280p. It would now be worth the option holder exercising his option and the shares held by the writer would be called away at a price of 260p.

The investor would 'lose' the stock, but make a higher return. This return would comprise, as before, of the option premium plus the dividend (assuming this is received before exercise), but in addition the writer would also have the benefit of a gain in the underlying shares of 20p from the original buying price to the exercise price. The denominator remains the same, making the 'if-called' return:

$$\frac{10+2+20}{240-10} = 13.9\%$$

This works out in this example at 55.6% on the same annualised basis.

Looked at in this way, writing options no longer looks quite as risky as it may at first appear. The drawback is that working out the same return if the shares fall sharply is less easy, since the writer may be faced with an overall loss on the holding even after allowing for the receipt of the option premium. However, in adopting the covered-write strategy the investor is still better off than he would have been had the option not been written and the shares simply held regardless.

For those with a neutral view on the market and a list of stocks which they are prepared to hold (if need be) as long term investments irrespective of shorter term market fluctuations, covered call writing makes sense.

Covered Put Writing
The 'covered' aspect involved in writing puts refers to the situation where the investor is perfectly happy to be assigned the stock if the put is exercised, and has the cash available to be able to fund the purchase. Put writing may well be undertaken in conjunction with an existing holding in the underlying stock, where the writer is perfectly happy to add to the holding if need be at a price below the current market price.

If for instance the investor is a holder of 10,000 XYZ shares, currently priced at 242p, and is happy to add a further 5,000 shares to this holding if the shares can be bought at say 230p, writing five 240 puts at 10p achieves this objective.

The advantages of writing puts, or indeed with writing any option, is that the premium received on the option serves to enhance portfolio performance and that the passage of time works in the writer's favour as the time value of the option decreases as it moves closer to expiry.

The disadvantages are that the potential for loss is theoretically unlimited (to zero) while, as illustrated in the case of the call, closing the position and re-establishing a more suitable one requires precise timing and judgement and is expensive.

Just as a written call can establish a potential selling price higher than the present share price, so a written put can be used to establish a potential buying price below the current share price.

Equivalent Strategies - Appraising Option Pricing

It should already be clear that option prices are not arrived at by chance. Though ultimately governed by supply and demand, premiums on options bear a close relationship to the price of the underlying stock, the time to expiry, and the volatility of the underlying shares. If substantial anomalies occur from the theoretical value ascribed to an option, arbitrage in the market ought quickly to iron it out.

Similarly, call and put prices for the same stock are not determined in isolation from each other. The relationship between the prices of the respective calls and puts and the price of the underlying stock can be assessed by comparing the prices implied by what are called 'equivalent' or 'synthetic' strategies.

These use a different combination of transactions from a straightforward option purchase or sale to arrive at the same risk profile as the simpler transaction. The method is to combine a position in the underlying stock with an equivalent position in the contrary option. As we saw in the example of Software Investments in Chapter 5:

- A bought call is equivalent (in terms of profit/loss potential) to combining bought stock and a bought put.

Similarly:

- A written call is equivalent to combining sold stock and a written put.

- A bought put is equivalent to combining sold stock and a bought call.

- A written put is equivalent to combining bought stock and a written call.

It can be seen intuitively that there is both symmetry and logic underlying these relationships, and this is confirmed by a comparison of the respective call and put prices for the same expiry date.

Imagine, for instance, that Wintergreen Pharmaceuticals plc shares are at 254p. The July 240 calls are 25p (ie. 14p intrinsic value + 11p time value) and the July 240 puts are 6p (all time value). Combining the stock price and the put price gives a composite price of 260p (the 254p share price plus the 6p cost of the put) or 20p above the exercise price of 240p. The effective purchase price of the stock through the straightforward purchase of a call is 265p. Therefore the call option is relatively overpriced.

Similarly combining selling the stock and buying the call to replicate the put would give an 'out' price of 229p (254p minus the 25p cost of the call), whereas the put price allows an effective selling level of 234p (the exercise price minus the cost of the put) and is therefore the better bargain.

Such calculations should be treated with some care. The spread between bid and offer prices can be sizeable in options and, in the above examples, dealing costs have been ignored. In addition, in the case of positions which involve the purchase of stock, it is obvious that the carrying cost of laying out the full price of the stock as opposed to just the option must be borne in mind. This can easily add a few pennies to the cost of the strategy.

Assuming an interest rate of 7%, on an option with three months to run and the underlying share at 254p, the carrying cost in the synthetic call strategy would be 4.45p. In the example above, this would account for virtually the whole of the disparity between the price of the option and the cost of the synthetic strategy.

Summary

1. An option writer is a trader whose initial (opening) transaction is the sale of an option.

2. UNCOVERED OPTION WRITING HAS THE POTENTIAL TO RESULT IN UNLIMITED LOSSES AND SHOULD NOT BE UNDERTAKEN.

3. Covered call writing involves writing options against an existing shareholding of similar or greater size than that implied by the option trade. In the case of covered writing of puts, by definition the investor will have sufficient cash to cope with the circumstances that the put is exercised and the underlying stock must be bought from the option holder.

4. Option writers receive, and keep under all circumstances, the premium paid by the option buyer. The option writer hopes for little volatility in the price of the shares concerned. Time works in favour of the option writer and against the option holder.

5. Option writing can be used as a legitimate portfolio strategy in a number of ways. When expecting stable markets, it may enable holders of the underlying stock to generate additional portfolio income. Returns can be attractive whether or not the option is exercised by the holder.

6. If the price rises marginally above the exercise price there is no guarantee that the writer will be called upon to meet his obligations, particularly if the option is some way away from expiry. Option holders may hang on to their options in the hope of a bigger gain.

7. Option writing is 'margined'. Those writing options are called upon to deposit with their broker sufficient funds or acceptable collateral ('margin') to ensure they will be financially capable of fulfiling the obligations of the option contract under all circumstances.

8. It is possible to combine positions in options and underlying stock which replicate the risk profile of a straightforward option purchase or sale. These are called synthetic strategies. They can be viewed as a way of assessing whether option prices are fair or not. Bid-offer spreads, dealing costs, and the cost of financing a position in the underlying stock, must all be taken into account when comparing these strategies.

SEVEN

INDEX OPTIONS

So far in this book we have looked at the market for options in individual stocks. However, most options exchanges in the world offer options on the leading stock market index for their market. In LIFFE's case, the main index option contracts offered are on the FTSE 100 index.

This chapter looks at the mechanics of index options, index construction and how it impacts on trading, who trades index options and why, and various other issues connected with index options. Although the mechanics are slightly different, trading index options involves similar strategy calculations to those done for normal equity options. These are covered in other chapters.

What are Index Options

As was mentioned in Chapter One, since an option is a simple contractual device, it is theoretically possible to create one based on virtually anything. And although numerically speaking most options traded in London are based on individual shares, the turnover in index options is well above that of all the individual equity options put together. It is, however, largely a professional's market. Individual equity options have traditionally proved more popular with the private investor, and this is likely to remain the case.

One reason for this is that equity options are easier to understand. Individual equity options have the characteristic that they respond to changes in the price of shares in one underlying company. It will have easily measured assets, liabilities, cash flow, and profits in its balance sheet profit and loss account. By contrast index options are based on something more abstract: that is, a mathematical device used to produce a single number to represent the market as a whole.

However, as investors in Polly Peck and Maxwell Communications will know to their cost, profit and loss statements and balance sheets are not always what they seem. Making trading decisions on the basis of the performance of a large basket of shares should be inherently less risky than making them on the basis of just one share. This is because risk is spread. Because of the way market indices are

---

KEY TERMINOLOGY

Arithmetic Index - An index calculated by adding together the values for a number of constituents and dividing by the total number. The FTSE 100 Index is an arithmetic index, weighted according to the market capitalisation of its constituents.

Geometric Index - An index calculated by multiplying the values of its 'n' constituents and taking the 'n'th root of the resulting figure. The FT Ordinary (30 share) index is a geometric index.

Cash Settlement - Deals in index options are settled into cash rather the underlying index constituents, on the basis of a fixed cash amount per index point.

EDSP - Exchange Delivery Settlement Price. This forms the basis of settlement for index contracts on expiry and is calculated on the basis of an average every 15 seconds of the values seen in the last 20 minutes of trading immediately prior to expiry. This device is used to avoid anomalies which might result from large, one-off transactions in the run-up to expiry.

European/American Exercise Style - Index options are available on LIFFE in a choice of exercise styles. American-style is where the option can be exercised on any business day up to and including expiry. LIFFE equity options are American-style exercise. European-style is where exercise can only take place on the day of expiry.

Arbitrageur - A trader who attempts to exploit a small disparity in value between and index and its constituents by large scale transactions selling one and buying the other.

---

constructed, a disaster in any one constituent will not permanently drag down the index with it.

This reduction in risk also means, however, that lower returns are likely. Skilled equity investors look to outperform the market by picking shares whose prospects are better than the market as a whole, or whose potential has not been recognised. Looking at the options market as an extension of the underlying equity market, the same should be true of individual traded options.

Percentage movements in some underlying shares are likely to be greater than the index as a whole, and therefore the potential for gain in the appropriate options series could also be that much better. Of course just as some stocks will outperform the index, others by definition will not and the performance of the totality of equity options is not likely to differ significantly from those based on the index. The point is that the opportunity is there for the investor to use skill to pick those individual shares and equity options which are likely to do better.

There is another major difference between equity options and index options. If an investor deals in an equity option, if it is exercised the underlying shares change hands. If this were replicated in the case of an index option, the need would be for shares in each of the index constituents to be delivered in precise proportions to each other.

Since this would be at worst impossible and at best unwieldy, the system has been devised whereby the option is exercisable into cash on the basis of a fixed amount per index point. This is simply a mechanism by which, if exercised or at expiry, a cash difference reflecting the price change in the underlying index changes hands, rather than the constituent securities themselves.

In fact, as with equity options, prior to expiry most open positions in a particular index options series will have been closed, with the option sold in the market for a profit or loss.

The cash settlement system is only provided for index option contracts and its rationale is obvious. Any other form of settlement would be unsatisfactory in terms of its inconvenience, the time it would take to administer, the expense it would involve (buying and or selling individual index constituents in precise quantities), consequent reduced liquidity for the index option (few people would bother to trade it given the hassles involved), and the potential for market distortion.

This latter point is particularly important. Since an option requires the holder to make or take delivery of the underlying security if the contract is exercised, this process would be capable of abuse by other market participants if it became known that a particular index constituent was in short supply and was required to fulfil the terms of a particular index option. The result might be the artificial driving up (or down) of the price of a particular share or group of shares. In the US, for instance, it is interesting to note that regulators stipulate cash settlement as one of the conditions for the listing of an exchange traded index futures or options contract.

The importance of this can be judged by the fact that, even with the safeguard of cash settlement, there are occasional accusations levelled against particular securities houses that - driven by particular option positions - their market-making arms have attempted to move the index to a particular level or beyond as expiry nears.

LIFFE's FTSE 100 index options come with a choice of two exercise styles - American or European. This terminology is simply an historical convention and has nothing to do with the geographical origin of the investor, currencies or any other factor. American-style options can be exercised at any time up to and including the expiry date, whereas European-style can only be exercised on the expiry date itself.

Whereas individual equity options are normally American-style exercise, the alternatives are offered in the case of the index options and, if dealing in them, it is important to stipulate when giving the order to the broker which style of option is going to be involved.

Because of the restricted flexibility the European exercise style offers the holder (and consequently lower risk for the writer), premiums on these options are generally lower than their American-style counterparts.

The specifications of the two FTSE 100 index options is shown in *Figure 7* and *Figure 8* on pages 105 and 106 respectively.

Note from these tables the difference in expiry cycle and exercise prices between the American style exercise and the European style exercise. In addition, the intervals between strike prices is determined by the time to maturity of a particular expiry month and is either 50 or 100 index points (50 points the nearer the option gets to maturity). New exercise prices are introduced if the underlying index level exceeds the second highest or second lowest available exercise price. Of particular note too is the mechanism by which the calculation of the index value on the expiry date is arrived at.

Expiry takes place at 10.30 am of the last trading day and all contracts traded that day are settled at the EDSP (Exchange Delivery Settlement Price). This is a weighted average of the index value during the last 20 minutes of trading. For some years this was calculated on a minute-by-minute basis, with the value of the index taken each minute from 10.10am to 10.30am inclusive. The three highest and three lowest figures were excluded and the remaining 15 averaged to arrive at the value of the index on expiry. More recently, the average has been worked out by taking index values every 15 seconds over the same period of time. This experiment has proved cumbersome and LIFFE may soon move back to the old system. An example of how the EDSP is calculated (on the minute-by-minute basis) is shown in *Figure 9* on page 107.

As noted previously, this method of calculation is used in order to forestall the possibility that only large one-off transactions could exert undue influence on the expiry value and therefore the profit and/or loss on particular index futures and option positions.

Indices and How they are Calculated
Before looking at other aspects of index options, it is important to understand the background to index construction in general and that of the FTSE 100 index in particular.

It is obvious that stockmarket indices are intended to reflect the movement in the market as a whole and are designed to produce a benchmark figure with which the performance of individual stocks and indices relating to other markets can be compared.

FTSE Index Option (American Style Exercise)

Unit of trading	Valued at £10 per index point (eg. value £48,000 at 4800.0).
Expiry months	June and December plus such additional months that the four nearest calendar months are always available for trading.
Exercise/Settlement day	Exercise by 16.31 on any business day, extended to 18.00 for expiring series on the Last Trading Day. Settlement Day is the first business day after the day of Exercise/Last Trading Day.
Last Trading Day	10.30 Third Friday of the Expiry Month.*
Quotation	Index Points.
Minimum Price Movement (Tick size and value)	0.5 (£5.00)
Trading hours	08.35 – 16.10

Contract Standard
Cash settlement based on a Daily Settlement Price for non-expiring series or the Exchange Delivery Settlement Price for expiring series.

Daily Settlement Price
The Daily Settlement Price is the equivalent of the FTSE 100 Index level at 16.10.

Exchange Delivery Settlement Price (EDSP)
The EDSP is based on the average level of the FTSE 100 Index between 10.10 and 10.30 on the Last Trading Day.

Option Premium
Option Premium is payable in full by the buyer on the business day following a transaction.

Exercise Price and Exercise Price Intervals
The interval between exercise prices is determined by the time to maturity of a particular expiry month and is either 50 or 100 index points.

Introduction of new Exercise Prices
Additional exercise prices will be introduced on the business day after the underlying Index level has exceeded the second highest, or fallen below the second lowest, available exercise price.

* In the event of the third Friday not being a business day, the Last Trading Day shall normally be the last business day preceding the third Friday.

Figure 7: FTSE 100 Index Option (American Style) contract specification

FTSE 100 Index Option (European Style Exercise)

Unit of trading	Valued at £10 per index point (eg. value £48,000 at 4800.0).
Expiry months	March, June, September and December plus such additional months that the three nearest calendar months are always available for trading.
Exercise/Settlement day	Exercise by 18.00 for expiring series on the Last Trading Day. Settlement Day is the first business day after the Last Trading Day. (An option can be exercised on the Last Trading Day.)
Last Trading Day	10.30 Third Friday of the Expiry Month.*
Quotation	Index Points.
Minimum Price Movement (Tick size and value)	0.5 (£5.00)
Trading hours	08.35 − 16.10

Contract Standard
Cash settlement based on the Exchange Delivery Settlement Price.

Exchange Delivery Settlement Price (EDSP)
The EDSP is based on the average level of the FTSE 100 Index between 10.10 and 10.30 on the Last Trading Day.

Option Premium
Option Premium is payable in full by the buyer on the business day following a transaction.

Exercise Price and Exercise Price Intervals
The interval between exercise prices is determined by the time to maturity of a particular expiry month and is either 50 or 100 index points.

Introduction of new Exercise Prices
Additional exercise prices will be introduced on the business day after the underlying Index level has exceeded the second highest, or fallen below the second lowest, available exercise price.

* In the event of the third Friday not being a business day, the Last Trading Day shall normally be the last business day preceding the third Friday.

Figure 8: FTSE 100 Index Option (European Style) contract specification

Example of EDSP Calculation

Time on last trading day	Last 21 Index figures from 10.10 to 10.30	Exclude 3 of Highest (H) Lowest (L)	Remaining 15 Index figures
10.10	4556.9		4556.9
10.11	4557.5		4557.5
10.12	4558.4		4558.4
10.13	4559.0	4559.0(H)	
10.14	4558.9		4558.9
10.15	4559.3	4559.3(H)	
10.16	4559.0	4559.0(H)	
10.17	4558.6		4558.6
10.18	4557.9		4557.9
10.19	4557.2		4557.2
10.20	4555.8		4555.8
10.21	4554.4		4554.4
10.22	4553.6		4553.6
10.23	4552.7		4552.7
10.24	4552.4		4552.4
10.25	4551.6		4551.6
10.26	4551.2		4551.2
10.27	4550.9		4550.9
10.28	4550.5	4550.5(L)	
10.29	4550.0	4550.5(L)	
10.30	4550.0	4550.0(L)	

Total of 15 middle quotes	68328.0
Average of 15 middle quotes	4555.2
Rounded to nearest 0.5	4555.0
Final EDSP	**4555.0**

Example of Cash Settlement
In August an investor buys 2 FTSE 100 Index Sept 4500 call options (SEI) at 35 - a cost of £700 ignoring dealing expenses. On expiry, September's EDSP is set at 4555.0. The contracts are exercised and the holder receives £1,100 (£10 x 2 contracts x 55 points) on the day after expiry. His profit on the transaction is thus £400 (ie. £1,100 − £700).

Note: These calculations were arrived at by the 'minute-by-minute' basis. Currently the EDSP is calculated on the basis of reading every 15 seconds.

Figure 9: Example of how EDSP is calculated

All major stock markets and most minor ones have indices which attempt to mirror their underlying performance. Broadly speaking, the more developed the stock market, the more indices will be available. In the USA, the Dow Jones and Standard and Poors (S&P) indices have long been established as market benchmarks, and a variety of other indices have been spawned relating to their different sub-groups.

For instance there are sub-groups of the Dow Jones Index which cover Utilities and Transport, as well as Financials and other groups, while the S&P market index is split into a number of sector groups. This index can be broadly compared with the FTSE All Share Index and its component sector indices, with which UK readers will be familiar.

In the UK, indices have been calculated since the 1930s. The most venerable is the FT 30, which began life then. The FTSE All Share Index and its sub-groups began in 1962, originally as a joint effort between the *Financial Times* and the Institute of Actuaries. Recently, however, ownership and administration of the indices has been taken over by a separate company, FTSE International, jointly owned by the FT and the London Stock Exchange. The Institute of Actuaries' influence continues in its membership of the committee which vets index construction and membership.

It is worth touching at this point on the broad differences in index construction, since this has had an important bearing on the development of new indices, and on futures and options products based on them.

All stock market indices are averages of the values of their constituent parts, but there are different ways of calculating them. The differences boil down to: first, whether the index should be an arithmetic average or a geometric average; and second, how it should be weighted.

The FT 30 index, the oldest-established, is a straight unweighted geometric average of the 30 shares which are its constituents. This means that each of the share prices concerned is multiplied together and the 30th root of the resulting number taken to arrive at the index value. This is a comparatively simple calculation but has its drawbacks. The minor drawback is that no account is taken of the differing size of index constituents. Companies of different sizes, in terms of sales, profits and market capitalisation, are treated identically in terms of their influence on the index.

Secondly, and more importantly, geometric indices find it difficult to cope with corporate disasters, and the effect of these tends to be magnified in the index calculation. In theory at least, if an index constituent goes bust, or its shares are suspended, its stock market value is zero and, since this is multiplied in as part of the index calculation, the value of the index would be zero at that point too. This drawback was highlighted in the later stages of the 1974/75 bear market when index constituents had be hurriedly replaced to avoid a disaster of this type.

It is obvious that an index which has the capacity to perform in this way is inherently unsuitable for use in tandem with futures and options contracts.

The FTSE All Share Index (then known as the FT-Actuaries All Share Index) and its component parts were created in the early 1960s to provide a more reliable and broader-based alternative to the FT 30.

The FTSE All Share Index and its components are arithmetic averages, weighted by market capitalisation. In other words the stockmarket value of each company (its outstanding shares multiplied by its share price) is added together and the result divided by the total number of constituents in the index. The resulting index value is calculated once each day and is clearly influenced both by any additional shares which companies may issue and by changes in each share price. This principle, of weighting-by-market-capitalisation, is followed through into the calculation of sub-sector indices too.

Such an index is clearly a more suitable variable on which to base futures and options products. However, the sheer number of companies taken in by the index, currently in the region of 900, covering an estimated 98% of the stock market's overall value, suggest that its calculation on a real-time basis (as is required for futures and option products) would be unwieldy.

Or at least that was how it was perceived in the early 1980's. Since that time the advent of sophisticated digital price feeds and the move by the stock market to an all-electronic pricing mechanism, as well as vast improvement in computing power might all suggest that calculating the All Share Index on a minute-by-minute basis is no longer particularly daunting.

However, the start of the financial futures market in 1983 gave rise for calls to create an index on which futures and options products could be based, and which would be capable of real-time dissemination. Neither the FT 30 nor the All Share index, for the reasons described above, were deemed suitable.

The main reason for the trouble taken over the precise construction of the index is that to act as the underlying security for a futures or options contract, the market being represented should be deep, liquid and accessible, with prices easily available to futures and options market participants. In other words, the index should move smoothly throughout the trading day, reflecting the actions of large numbers of buyers and sellers across a broad range of stocks.

In addition it is necessary that the construction of the index be such that the derivative product (future or option) based on it will be suitable for the needs of a broad spectrum of likely market users. It must be easy to trade, for traders. It must not be so broad an index as to preclude the possibility of arbitrage. This is the process of buying or selling the future against an simultaneous opposite transaction in the underlying basket of shares to profit from a discrepancy in the price. Too big a basket of shares makes the exercise too cumbersome and costly relative to the price discrepancies that might occur.

Yet it should also be broad enough to be used by fund managers as an acceptable hedge. The fund manager wants to be sure, if buying a range of shares to add to his portfolio but dealing in an equivalent number of options or futures to hedge against a possible market setback, that the index on which the hedge is based will replicate accurately the performance of his portfolio under the same conditions.

The result of the reconciling of these different objectives was the creation of the FTSE 100 share index, a joint venture between the *Financial Times* and the Stock Exchange, calculated by the Stock Exchange on a minute-by-minute basis throughout the trading day.

The index was formally launched in January 1984, with the baseline of 1000 being the value on 31st December 1983. Prior to its introduction it had been thoroughly back-tested to 1978 by the London Business School to determine how well it correlated with other market indicators over a variety of stock market conditions.

The FTSE 100 Index ('Footsie') and Index Options

As its name implies, the index is constructed from 100 of the largest UK listed blue chip companies as an arithmetic average weighted according to market capitalisation. This means that a 5% change, say, in a company with a market capitalisation of £1500m, will have a proportionately greater impact on the change in the index value than a 5% change in a stock with a market capitalisation of £1000m. The 100 companies represent about 72% of the capitalisation of the market and the index is therefore likely to be a good market proxy for hedging purposes, whilst remaining small enough, with its 100 stocks, to be used for arbitrage should opportunities arise.

One important feature, from the standpoint of user of the index futures and options markets, is that the rules for the administration of the index to take account of various events that can affect its value are pre-determined and administered by an independent committee comprised of representatives from the *Financial Times*, the London Stock Exchange, market users, LIFFE, and the Institute of Actuaries. The committee meets quarterly, or more frequently if necessary.

Its procedures cover rules for inclusion and exclusion of particular companies, and what happens in the event of take-overs, rights issues, new issues, and suspensions.

In the case of the procedure for inclusion in the list, the ideal is for the index to contain the largest 100 companies by market capitalisation at any one time. However, because this is capable of changing on a daily basis, the list is reviewed quarterly and a 90/110 rule adopted.

This means that any company whose market capitalisation has risen to the 90th position or above is automatically included. Any that has fallen below 110th place is excluded.

Constituents which are then between 101 and 110 may be removed to make room for the stock or stocks which have a higher capitalisation. In addition there is a reserve list of stocks to take account of changes which may need to be made between reviews because of takeovers or suspensions.

Changes to the list are publicised in advance and are normally implemented on the first business day following the expiry of the FTSE 100 index futures and options contracts (normally the Monday following the third Friday of the months of March, June, September and December).

In the case of mergers and takeovers, the vacant place is filled from the reserve list. This applies even if the takeover has been of one index constituent by another.

It is only rarely that a newly floated company will be large enough to qualify for inclusion in the index. In these instances, however (which occurred, for example, following the British Gas privatisation and more recent building society and insurance company demutualisations), the new stock will qualify for automatic membership of the index. In these instances, the change is normally made from the date of the next quarterly meeting. Membership of the index requires a substantial market capitalisation. At the time of writing, the threshold for a company to qualify for automatic inclusion in the index was a total market value for its shares of in the region of £3bn.

If an index constituent is suspended for whatever reason, once the suspension has lasted beyond midday the following business day, the Committee will convene a meeting to decide whether or not it should be removed from the list . This will depend on the circumstances of the suspension.

If it appears to be temporary, the index will continue to be calculated on the basis of the market value of the stock at the suspension price. If it has not been relisted by the time ten days are up, if not already removed it will deleted from the index on the eleventh day at a value of 1p and replaced by a constituent from the reserve list.

For obvious reasons, companies which are subsidiaries of larger existing constituents are excluded from the list, as are overseas registered companies and those with large controlling shareholders owning more than 75% of the issued share capital.

The result of these rules is that it is entirely predictable at any one time which the index constituents are, what the procedure is for changing them under any eventuality, and what stocks will be on the reserve list on the basis of their ranking in terms of market capitalisation.

In addition the 'Footsie' has a close and reasonably predictable statistical relationship with the other main indices, measured by the correlation coefficient of one with the other (the extent to which a movement in one variable is 'explained' by the movement in the other). For example, the FTSE 100 index is over 99%

correlated with the All Share Index and with the FTSE 350 (with which it shares 100 constituents). The correlation with the FTSE 250 (whose constituents are those ranking from 101 to 350 by market capitalisation) is lower - around 90%.

Although these relationships are close, there are differences in the composition of the indices which affect performance over the longer term. One is that smaller companies tend to perform differently to their larger counterparts, alternately coming into and going out of favour. Over an extended period of time, however, small companies - as measured by indices such as the Hoare Govett Smaller Companies Index or the FTSE SmallCap - have tended to outperform the FTSE 100.

Compared to those companies included in the broader indices, FTSE100 constituents - while not immune from it - are on the whole less likely to be subject to takeover and merger activity, simply because of their sheer size. It is worth noting also that the FTSE 100 index has significantly different sector composition to the All Share Index, with a preponderance of consumer stocks and financials, and a lower weighting towards capital goods, oil and gas, and investment trusts. This disparity has been further exaggerated by the inclusion of recently demutualised financial institutions in the FTSE 100 Index.

Evaluation and Use of Index Options

The evaluation of index options is conducted in precisely the same way as for normal equity options on the basis of tried and tested theoretical valuation models. These take into account a number of factors to arrive at the 'correct' price for a particular option. These factors were listed and examined in more detail in Chapter Two. To recap, the components of an option's price are:

- Whether it is a put or a call.

- The exercise price

- The price of the underlying instrument (ie. security or index)

- The volatility of the underlying instrument

- The length of time to the option's expiry

- Market interest rates

- Dividends on the underlying instrument

In the case of normal equity options the term 'instrument' refers to the underlying equity share in question. In the case of an index option it refers to the FTSE 100 index and parameters related to it. It is, for instance, quite easy to calculate the likely aggregate flow of dividend payments for the components of the index on a month by month or week-by-week basis.

In calculating what might be a fair price for an option, it is clear that some element of forecasting of the future flow of dividends is required. This is comparatively simple to do for an individual equity option, although it is less certain that the forecast will be a correct one.

For an index option, the aggregate of consensus forecasts for each constituent company is likely to be close to the eventual outturns and less subject to sharp variations than those for individual shares.

Who Uses Index Options and How?

The concepts introduced in Chapter Two relating to in-the-money, out-of-the-money, and at-the-money options, time-value and intrinsic value, can be applied in exactly the same way to index options, as can the trading strategies for options outlined elsewhere in this book.

It is perhaps worth at this point enumerating the different users of the index options market and how options are employed to meet their objectives.

This is important to the private investor because it may help to understand who the professional users of the market are, and how and why they behave as they do, and the impact of their actions on the rest of the market.

The main users of index options are generally fund managers, market-makers, traders and arbitrageurs.

In the case of a fund manager, index options are used primarily for the purpose of maintaining the value of a portfolio in a declining market, maximising its returns, and improving performance through greater ease of asset reallocation. Those fund managers who use options are, for instance, typically active as covered writers.

Market-makers on occasion will wish to hedge the overall exposure of a diversified trading book against the possibility of a sudden market fall.

Traders with a strong view of where the market is headed can use index options as a way of achieving maximum gearing for a given level of capital investment, with the proviso that, if their view proves incorrect, their investment is at risk.

Arbitrageurs look to exploit pricing anomalies between the index derivative and the underlying constituent shares, as well as between different combinations of puts, calls and underlying security.

The advantages of using futures and options in these ways (rather than dealing in the underlying stocks) are lower transaction costs (narrower bid-offer spreads and lower commissions) and ease and simplicity of dealing. In addition, using options offers an ability to go short of the market (ie bet on a fall in the index), for instance by buying index put options.

Another advantage of using options to adjust the risk profile of a portfolio is that, although the underlying exposure to the market can be effectively reduced through hedging, since the actual portfolio is undisturbed the flow of dividends from the constituent stocks continues to accrue.

The activities of these professional market users all contribute to the liquidity of the traded options and futures markets and ensure both a high level of liquidity and the efficient pricing of the various risks involved.

Summary

1. Just as the investor can deal in options based on the shares in individual companies, so there are also options available on the FTSE 100 index.

2. The FTSE 100 index is arithmetic average of the stockmarket capitalisation of its constituents. There are strict rules governing which shares are included and the frequency of any changes to the list.

3. 'Footsie' options are available in both American and European exercise styles, that is either to be exercised at any time up to expiry, or on the day of expiry only. Both styles are exercisable into cash rather than into the underlying basket of shares, on the basis of a fixed cash sum per index point.

4. Compared to normal equity options, index options are also available with a bigger range of strike prices (normally in 50-point or 100-point intervals) and with an extended number of expiry months, normally the three or four nearest individual months, plus the three and six months beyond that. The expiry cycle differs for American and European exercise styles.

5. Because they represent a broad cross section of shares, indices tend to be less volatile than ordinary shares. This is reflected in index option premiums. However, index options can be valued in exactly the same way as ordinary equity options, and similar strategies can be employed.

EIGHT

USING COMPUTER MODELS FOR VALUING OPTIONS

Previous chapters have looked at the definitions and terminology of equity and index options, and how they can be used in some simple strategies. Before going on to examine more complex uses of options, we look at how computer software can be used to make the task of valuing and monitoring options easier.

If this sounds daunting, it should be remembered that using computers in this way is no substitute for the judgement needed to work out correctly when a particular option strategy is suitable and when the market, or a particular option stock, should be avoided.

Computers do not replace good judgement about the market, merely provide the investor with an additional tool. The computer programs described do not indicate when is an appropriate moment to trade, or what type of strategy is best under particular circumstances.

They can assist in the process of estimating the appropriate price of the option because of movements in the price of the underlying shares, or because of changes in volatility, and likely profit or loss outcomes under various alternative scenarios.

Where some software can also assist, however, is in the rapid estimation of historic and implied volatility, and so help the investor to make a judgement about whether, on the basis of these measures, an option looks cheap or dear. Other parameters which are of use in a trading environment, such as the option delta and percentage gearing to changes in the underlying share price, can also be calculated.

Requirements, Practicalities and Cost
System requirements for options valuation programmes are not in themselves particularly demanding. A conventional 486 or Pentium PC will cope with all the necessary calculations comfortably. Most packages are 'Windows' based. There are a few commonly available programs for Apple Mac users.

115

Basic stand-alone option pricing and valuation programs use comparatively modest amounts of system memory for their operation, normally under 1MB.

However, option pricing and strategy models are more often than not used in conjunction with, or even supplied as part of more comprehensive technical analysis packages which chart the movement of underlying share prices and various indicators derived from them. The use of these charts and indicators in formulating option strategies is examined in Chapter 10.

Technical analysis packages like this tend to take up slightly greater amounts of system memory and storage space. A low-priced chart package running under Windows 3.1 might occupy around 1.5MB, while a more sophisticated one, running in Windows 95, would occupy about 7.5MB of hard disk space. All packages like this work better with faster processors.

The most important aspect of option software supplied as part of technical analysis packages is that they invariably include a mechanism by which daily share price data is captured and stored for future use.

This is done either by capturing the share price data on teletext services, through dialling up a commercial share price database, via downloading prices from some other price service such as 'Market Eye' or Prestel, or increasingly via a daily email. These choices will be examined in greater detail in Chapters 10 and 11.

The relevance of this from the option investor's standpoint is that linking a technical analysis package, with its accompanying daily-updated share price datafiles, to an option pricing and valuation model means that the calculation of historic volatility can be done automatically from the stored history of share prices. This makes things slightly easier, but it is worth remembering that many of the cheaper technical analysis charting packages can calculate historic volatility and graph it over time.

This can be an important pointer to where future volatility might be heading, which is one of the variables the option buyer is interested in. So in many respects a combination of one of these technical analysis packages with a basic option pricing calculator may be all that is required.

Stand-alone option pricing calculators are available free online at several web sites or in a downloadable form as shareware. Prices range from a few pounds up to around £100. Some brokers supply software to their option clients either free of charge or for a nominal fee.

Longer established software firms like Synergy Software, Fairshares and Indexia Research offer option pricing modules as optional extras to some of their packages. Professional option traders tend to use more complex systems that work from real-time prices. LIFFE's *Directory of Further Information* on equity and index options contains details of software packages for option pricing and technical analysis and their capabilities ('functionality' in software jargon) and cost.

The use of the charting and technical analysis aspects of products of this type is examined more closely in Chapter 10.

Finally, it should be stressed that option valuation programmes do not chart option prices over time. There are differences of opinion about whether or not this is a sensible exercise to do. Some technical analysts claim to be able to see patterns in option prices which can enable trading judgements to be made, but professionals in the market almost invariably work more on the basis of the systems described above (or sophisticated variants of them).

The following sections cover in turn the different functions of typical option valuation models available to the private investor and examine the uses to which they can be put. It should be stressed, however, that the only effective way to learn about these packages and how they can help in making trading judgements is actually to use them for oneself.

The investor may wish to wait until he or she has greater familiarity with the options market before buying a package of this type, or else may feel that learning to use such a package is an essential pre-condition to being able to trade effectively. My own view inclines to the latter, but would-be option investors should not feel inhibited about dealing in the market simply because they are not experts in using computer software.

Making the initial judgement about the position of an underlying share in the context of the market as a whole is not necessarily something which can be reduced to a mechanical, computer-driven system.

What follows is based on the author's use of a few different option packages, some of which are used as illustrations. No recommendation of one system over another is intended, nor should it be implied.

All option packages like this fulfil one or both of two basic functions. One is the facility to value a single option in detail, and to draw charts based on its characteristics. The second is to chart particular strategies. In the more sophisticated packages, option transactions can be stored so that profit and loss profiles for alternative 'what if' strategies can be built up. These two functions are considered in turn below.

Valuing an Option

Most option software packages work on the basis that certain basic details can be programmed into the system in advance or entered at the outset before any price related information is input. These include expiry dates for future expiry months, the exercise price of the option, whether or not it is a call or put, and the nature of the underlying instrument.

This brings one to an important point. Option valuation packages can be used to value any option. This is irrespective of whether it is an option on a stock, an index, a future, or a commodity. In the case of equity options, the user is not confined to valuing simply those options available on LIFFE. In theory, any option, quoted or otherwise, can be valued using such packages - provided the main parameters of underlying price, exercise price, time to expiry and volatility are known or can be estimated.

As an example, the screen shot shows the basic data entry screen for Intelligent Research System's Option Evaluator package.

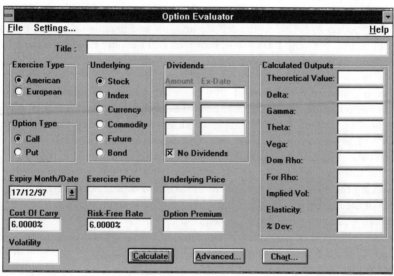

Figure 10: Basic data entry screen.

The pre-entered and/or default values are all that are shown on the screen at this stage. These are: the assumption that the option is a call; that the option has American-style exercise; that the underlying instrument is a stock; the nearest expiry date; the assumed risk-free interest rate and cost of carry; and the assumption - indicated by the cross in the checkbox - that no dividend payments are to be taken into account or are due during the life of the option. These can be changed as and when necessary.

Other variables that need to be entered are the name of the option series (at the top of the screen), the exercise price of the option, the price of the underlying and price of the option. If this is done and the 'calculate' button pressed using the mouse, the other cells are calculated automatically. If the price of the option is entered, the system will automatically calculate implied volatility. Alternatively, if a move to a particular level of volatility is expected, this can be entered in the volatility cell and the system will calculate the implied price of the option.

Inputting the variables for, say, the Allied Domecq July 550 calls and then pressing the button to perform the calculations produces a screen which looks like this:

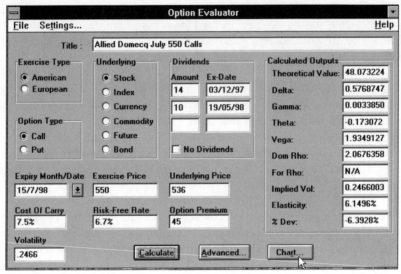

Figure 11: Input variables for Allied Domecq July 550.

This requires a little further elaboration:

■ *Call/Put:* The system enables the user to choose either a call or put option as required. The system defaults to a call.

■ *Underlying:* The system enables the user to choose between a stock option (ie. one on an equity), index option, option on a future, bond, currency or commodity as required. The system defaults to a stock.

■ *Interest Rate:* This item enable the user to specify the interest rates to be used in the option pricing calculation. As will be remembered from earlier chapters, the level of interest rates is an important feature in the pricing of options. The system enables the rate which the investor could obtain through investing surplus cash in a risk-free form to be entered.

■ The system also takes care of dividends. Either enter the gross dividend yield on the underlying shares in the 'cost of carry' box, leaving the 'dividends' checkbox unchanged. Or enter the precise amount and timing of expected dividends during the life of the option. In this instance, leave the cost of carry box at the default value.

■ *Calculation Method:* There are various methods of calculating option prices. The mathematical technicalities of these are not unduly important for the user. The Black-Scholes method is the most commonly used for valuing European-style options. The binomial (Cox-Ross-Rubinstein) method is normally used for pricing options with American-style exercise. These different choices are selected automatically.

■ *Expiry Date:* Choosing the expiry month (in this instance July) produces the precise date of option expiry. Some option pricing models also display (or require to be entered) the number of days remaining to expiry.

This covers the variables which are normally input into the screen. The items calculated by the model are the theoretical option price, the implied volatility, and the option's delta, gamma, theta, vega, rho, (the so-called 'greeks') and the option's elasticity.

Some of these terms have been covered before. To recap, the **volatility** is a measure of the variability of the share price. Expressed as a percentage, it represents the percentage change either side of the current share price beyond which the price is unlikely to move roughly two-thirds of the time. Higher volatility means higher option prices, other things being equal. Implied volatility is the level of volatility suggested by the market price of the option.

The option **delta** is the absolute amount by which the price of the option will move for a 1p change in the price of the underlying shares. In this case, it can be seen that the delta value is approximately 0.5768. This means that for every penny movement up or down in the price of the shares, the option price will move by slightly more than half a penny.

The option **gamma** measures the rate of change in the delta value for a 1p change in the underlying price. In the example shown, the delta value with the underlying at 536p is (in round figures) 0.0034. The delta value with the underlying at 537p would be the original delta value plus the gamma value, in other words 0.5768 + 0.0034, or 0.5802.

Theta is the mathematical expression for the rate of decrease in time value of the option, expressed in pence. Hence, in this example, the option would, other things being equal, decrease in value by 0.17 per day, or approximately 1.2p per week.

Vega is the measure of an option's sensitivity to change in volatility - the amount by which an option price would move for each one percentage point change in volatility. In this case the value is 1.93, suggesting that a one point rise in volatility would lead to about a 2p change in the option price.

Rho is the option's sensitivity to changes in interest rates. For the purposes of most equity option trades, this value can be ignored.

Elasticity is the percentage change in the price of the option for a small percentage change in the underlying security. In the example, the elasticity of the option is 6.15. This means that a 1% change up or down in the underlying share price would produce a 6.2% change in the price of the option.

Using the information

It probably goes without saying that this information - especially delta, theta and vega - can be used as a ready reckoner when faced with changes in the underlying price and the elapsing of time. This software package, and a number of others, however, also take this information a stage further. In the case of the Option Evaluator, an additional screen allows the chart of the profit and loss diagram for the option trade to be drawn, and several other variables displayed, including the probability that option will be in-the-money at expiry, the likely profit, the maximum profit and maximum loss. These are shown in the illustration.

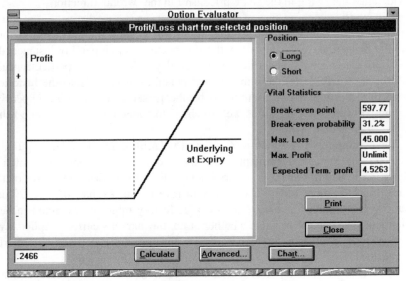

Figure 12: A Typical Profit and Loss chart.

The charts available on other packages may well be more comprehensive than this. Some, for instance, plot the option price against the time to expiry; the option price versus volatility; option price versus exercise price; option price versus interest rates; and option price versus dividend yield.

In fact, all these charts are doing is presenting in pictorial form the information which could be gained by doing a series of 'what if' calculations on the main calculation screen shown in *Figures 10* and *11*.

What is perhaps most important is to be aware of what questions to ask the model in particular circumstances, and to learn which variables to look at to determine the choice of an option which suits a particular risk profile.

Aside from most probably confirming that the market is more or less pricing the option correctly, a pricing model is of particular use in analysing volatility and producing a quick measure of the level of gearing or 'elasticity' present within a particular option. As stated previously, for those beginning option trading, deep in-the-money options with plenty of time to go to expiry are the least risky way of gaining a feel for the market.

Volatility is, however, arguably the most important variable. Choosing an option with a volatility that is low relative to its historic pattern is normally the best strategy for those buying options. The chances are that it will revert to the long term trend and provide the opportunity for a profitable move in the option, always provided that the swing in the share price isn't in the 'wrong' direction.

It is worth reiterating that many charting packages - as distinct from option pricing models - now include a feature which will graph a time series of historic volatility for periods of whatever length the user chooses to input. For instance, the trend over the last three years in, say, the 30-day volatility of a particular share could be measured to see how the current volatility level fits into the historical perspective. Features like this used to be the preserve of the more expensive charting software, so it is still as well to check that any system you intend using includes this facility.

The assumption that a long-term chart of volatility might be a better guide is based on the statistical principle that the more 'observations' on which a calculation is based, the more accurate and valid will be the calculation of the average and the more likely is volatility to revert to it. A chart of, say, 20-day volatility going back for three years of price history might be expected to be a better benchmark to use to judge whether or not the market's current implied level of volatility is about right, too high or too low than one constructed using a shorter time period.

But it is as well to remember that time is not on the side of the option purchaser in these situations. Even if volatility is unduly low, the likelihood of an eventual return to a more normal level has to be balanced against the certainty of erosion of time-value as the option moves towards expiry.

Another point to bear in mind when contemplating any profit that might be made from a volatility change on an option purchase is that account must be taken of the impact of the bid-offer spread on the option concerned, and the impact of dealing costs.

A concrete example should make this clear. Take the Allied July 550 calls used in the earlier example. Assume the volatility is 18%. If so, the value of the option with everything else unchanged would be 32p. Let's say you wish to buy on a volatility of 18% and sell on a volatility of 25%.

Now look at the bid-offer spread. This is 2p either side of the middle price when the price is in the low 30s but 3p if it is in the mid 40s. So if the actual middle price is 32p a buyer of the option would pay 34p. Assume the volatility moves up to 25% overnight. The appropriate middle price of the option would now be 45p according to the model, but the investor would only be able to sell for 42p. A theoretical mid price to mid price gain of 13p (40.6%) has been cut to 8p (23.5%) because of the impact of the spread.

Dealing costs would erode this gain further, the exact amount depending on the number of contracts purchased. If just one contract was bought, approximately a further 3p would have to be added to the buying price, cutting the gain to 13.5%. Even this assumes the closing bargain was commission free.

In addition, an increase in volatility can occur just as much from a sharp downward move in the shares as from a sharp rise. The investor must work out which of these eventualities is the most likely to occur and act accordingly. Examination of charts of the underlying share price can help in this regard. How this can be done is explored in Chapter 10.

The conclusion - that volatility should always be observed and compared when assessing whether a particular option is worth buying or not - is valid up to a point but must not simply be followed slavishly to the exclusion of any other variable. Anomalies may occur in volatility, but they are not necessarily themselves a sufficiently good reason for initiating a trade, nor a substitute for a sound judgement about the likely movement in the underlying stock and any changes in the market.

Investors will also be keen to observe the elasticity of a particular option as an indicator of the risk level they might be taking on with a particular option purchase. The point to remember here is the obvious one that elasticity or 'gearing' works in both directions. Although the 6.2:1 gearing suggested in the example shown in *Figure 11* looks mouthwatering if one contemplates the share price going up and buys a call, it looks hair-raising if the price is going down. A

10% fall in the Allied share price would produce a 62% fall in the value of the call option (other things being equal), to which has also to be added the erosion of time-value.

Lastly, 'what if' calculations can also be performed in the model using different assumptions of interest rate levels and dividend yields. Although the likely level of interest rates and dividends will normally be reflected in the market price of the options (ex-dividends do not normally affect options prices, for instance), abrupt and unexpected changes in either variable may create opportunities. Options market-makers have to react quickly to events such as dividend cuts or changes in interest rates and it is possible in these instances that options prices may get out of kilter, creating an opportunity for the astute investor.

Again, it is worth the investor remembering that he or she is not unique. The options market-makers and the mass of professional options traders will be equally alive to these opportunities and working from similar (or more sophisticated) computer models.

On the other hand, there are a sufficiently large number of options series for anomalies to occur, particularly in options which are comparatively infrequently traded. Here the small investor has an advantage compared to the professional, in that the size of his or her deal will not usually attract attention or move the price. Longer dated options might generally be considered more suitable for the private investor in any case, especially those which are in-the-money, and these tend to be among the more illiquid.

Simulating Strategies
One other important function of some option software, notably the modules that can be incorporated in technical analysis packages such as Synergy's OptionMaster or Indexia's Option Trader models, is that they can be used both to simulate and track strategies, or indeed to value existing multiple positions in particular options.

In systems of this type, the starting point is for the user to be presented with a screen that looks something like that shown in *Figure 13* on the opposite page.

	B S W	Quantity 1000's	Expiry Month	Exercise Price p	Call Put Inst.	Current Value Each p	Current Total Value £	Profit/ Current Cash £
No.								
1								
2								
3								
4								
5								
6								
7								
8								
9								
0	Current Position £				Total			

OptionMaster — Allied Domecq Security Strategy

Today's Date : 05/12/1997   Underlying Price :
Volatility % :   Interest Rate % : 9
Calculation Method : Black-Scholes   Dividend Rate % :

Figure 13: Allied Domecq - Security strategy screen.

This screen enables the user to enter either actual or proposed transactions to work out strategies related to them. Choices can be made between different option type, expiry month, exercise price, pricing model, and so on. Volatility can be entered manually or, in some instances, calculated by the system.

Software like this, like the option market itself, is flexible: strategies can be built up either through entering transactions (simulated or otherwise) on an ad hoc basis or through storing specific transaction types (buying an October 600 call, writing a January 650 put, and so on).

Short-cut commands allow new 'transactions' to be added quickly, specifying number of contracts, put or call, buy or write ('sell' is used only to close an existing transaction) exercise price, expiry month and so on.

Take as an example a simple simultaneous purchase of the April 550 call and put in Allied Domecq, with five contracts purchased in each case. This, as described in Chapter 5, is a strategy known as a 'straddle'. When the deals are entered into the system, they produce a screen something like the one in *Figure 14*.

		OptionMaster				**Allied Domecq Security Strategy**			
No.	B S W	Quantity 1000's	Expiry Month	Exercise Price p	Call Put Inst.	Current Value Each p	Current Total Value £	Profit/ Current Cash £	
1	B	5000	April	550	Call	25.241	1262	- 700	
2	B	5000	April	550	Put	26.417	1321	-1450	
3									
4									
5									
6									
7									
8									
9									
0	Current Position £			432.88(Profit)		Total	2583	-2150	

Today's Date : 05/12/1997	Underlying Price : 541
Volatility % : 20	Interest Rate % : 9
Calculation Method : Black-Scholes	Dividend Rate % : 5.2

Figure 14: Allied Domecq - April 550 straddle screen.

In this example, it can be seen that the system automatically assesses the value of the options on the basis of the information entered, and works out the initial profit/loss arising from entering the strategy. Systems of this type also allow for the production of a chart showing the profit/loss profile of the strategy. This is shown on *Chart 12*.

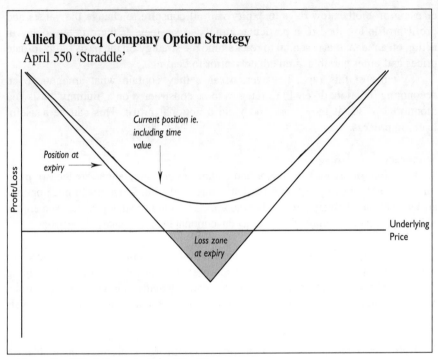

Chart 11: Allied Domecq Straddle Chart.

This chart resembles that of the straddle shown in Chapter 5, with the exception that the upper curved line shows the current position of the strategy, whereas the lower, more angular line is the position on expiry. In some charts, a vertical dotted line shows the current level of the underlying.

More complex strategies can be built up adding in further deals. A transaction in the underlying security can be added by selecting - in this case - 'inst' (ie. instrument) from the appropriate menu.

Using a system like this helps one understand the flexibility of the options market as a whole. Strategies can be tailored which produce a particular risk profile and reflect a particular market view, but they can also be amended as time goes by to reflect changes of view and movements in the market. Computerising the process makes it easier to establish quickly the potential profit and loss of different types of strategy and their risk profile - before dealing.

But remember, however, that option values and strategy calculations do not stand still. A small change in the option premium or the underlying price, or the elapsing of another few days to expiry will all conspire to change the values and profit profile ascribed to a particular simulated strategy. If there is any delay in acting on an idea, it is essential to re-examine the strategy on the basis of up-to-date prices and other variables immediately prior to dealing.

Systems of this type, however, because they contain what amounts to an accounting function, do enable strategies to be constructed on a 'dummy' basis and monitored to see if they work and yield a notional profit. This can be a useful learning process.

Summary

1. Valuation (or pricing) of options and option strategy simulations are the two main functions performed by option-related computer software. Programs to price options are available at relatively low cost but those used to simulate strategies may sometimes only be supplied in conjunction with a conventional technical analysis package.

2. It is important for the investor to have a system (normally using a modem or email) for capturing daily prices and storing price histories for the underlying option stocks. This is in order to be able to chart fluctuations in volatility over time. Volatility charting is available in a number (but not all) of technical analysis packages.

3. Well-featured stand-alone option pricing software is currently available for around £100 plus VAT. Prices for technical analysis software, including a volatility charting function, start at around £60. A typical data charge would be £10 per month, although this may include email and Internet access too.

4. Integral option pricing modules are normally only available as add-ons to the more expensive technical analysis packages, where prices can run into hundreds of pounds. More detail on different software packages and their capabilities and cost can be found in LIFFE's *Directory of Further Information*.

5. The value of option pricing packages is that they enable the user to calculate an option's volatility, gearing, and other variables with ease and to place these numbers in a chosen historical context, or compare them with the same variables in other options on the same stock, or with a similar option on a different stock.

6. The more expensive packages can produce profit and loss charts similar to those shown in other chapters, but with an added degree of sophistication and flexibility.

They also generally provide an accounting function which enables current transactions to be continually valued and past trades accorded.

7. Strategies can be simulated and actual transaction valuations built up easily and stored in the system. Packages of this type both mimic and amply illustrate the flexibility of the option market.

8   Software like this can also be used as a self-tutor to enable investors new to the market to gain confidence at selecting and and building up strategies while simulating the profit and loss consequences of them. This can be done prior to dealing.

9. No option software package should ever be seen as a substitute for making a proper informed judgement about the likely course of an option's underlying share price. That requires detailed study of the fundamentals of a company's business and the condition of the market, as well as some knowledge of the technical background to the shares. The technical analysis of share prices is considered in more detail in Chapter 10.

NINE

MORE COMPLEX OPTIONS STRATEGIES

In Chapters Four, Five and Six, some basic trading rules were outlined, along with simple options strategies. Chapter Eight looked at the ways in which computer-based analysis can help in formulating and monitoring options strategies. This chapter looks at the more complex strategies which option users may wish to use once they have gained confidence in their trading ability. The table of key words and definitions is on page 132.

One important feature of the options market is that there is a strategy to fit most views an investor can hold about the underlying shares or stockmarket concerned. Options investors can profit not only from a rising market, but also a falling one, and from volatility in the market. Neutral views about likely market action can also be accommodated, as can mildly bullish or mildly bearish opinions. The only requirement, as has been stressed before, is that the investor's view is a correct one in terms of its direction, magnitude and timing.

To recap, those with a bullish view would buy a call, those who are bearish would buy a put, those expecting higher volatility would buy a straddle or a strangle. Bulls prepared to countenance writing options would write a put. Bears would write calls. Those with a neutral view would write a straddle or a strangle. However, these are only a fraction of the possibilities open to option traders. Some of the more complex strategies are explored in greater detail below.

Spreads

Like straddles, the concept of a spread is another of the building blocks of options strategies. Spreads vary from the simple to the complex. Basic spreads are used when there is a reasonably confident view that a move in a particular direction will take place, but that the extent of the change is felt likely to be comparatively modest. Spreads involve buying and writing options in the same stock but with either different strike prices or different expiry dates.

Hence a **bull call spread** involves buying a call option with one strike price and writing (selling) a call option with a higher strike price in the same expiry month.

KEY TERMINOLOGY

Spread (or Vertical Spread) - a strategy which consists of buying one option and writing another with a higher or lower strike price but with the same expiry.

Bull Spread/ Bear Spread - in a bull spread the written option has a higher strike price than the bought one, in a bear spread a lower one. Spreads of the same type have similar risk profiles irrespective of whether calls or puts are used.

Calendar Spread - a spread created where the options involved have the same strike price but different expiry dates. The norm is for a near month option to be written, and a longer-dated option bought.

Diagonal Spread - a spread where the bought and written options each have both different exercise prices and expiry dates. It is normal for a near month option to be written and a longer-dated further out-of-the-money option to be bought.

Butterfly Spread - the combining of a bull spread and a bear spread with a common middle strike price.

Ratio Spread - the buying of one option and the writing of a greater number of contracts in a different, lower-priced option. For instance, buying one option at 16p but writing two options priced at 8p. A **Backspread** reverses the process, buying more of the lower-priced option and writing fewer of the higher-priced one.

The result of this is that the investor participates in a move in the underlying shares between the two strike prices but gains no further benefit in profit terms if the shares continue on above the higher of the two.

Spreads can be constructed at comparatively low cost or even a net credit, because the cost of the strategy comprises the payment of the premium for the bought call (or put), but the receipt of the premium on the written call (or put). The essence of bull spreads (and indeed other spread strategies), is that they offer known, but limited, profit and loss potential, and lower costs than a straightforward option purchase.

This is best illustrated with an example.

Example 9:

Moderately bullish view - A BULL CALL SPREAD.

VIEW: ICHS Investments is currently priced at 204p. It is 1st March and an investor believes that the shares, whose next results announcement is due in June, will rise gently in the run-up to the announcement. The investor wishes to take advantage of this without incurring a heavy outlay.

ACTION: buy 5 ICHS July 200 calls at 16p and write 5 ICHS July 220 calls at 8p. The net cost of the strategy is 8p per contract, or £400 in all (5 x 1,000 x 8p). The result of this will be that the investor will participate in any movement in ICHS's price above 208p (the lower of the two strike prices plus the net cost of the strategy) up to 220p. The maximum profit on the strategy is therefore 12p per share for an outlay of 8p.

WHAT HAPPENS NEXT: the investor's judgement proves correct and over the following eight weeks the share price of ICHS rises to 218p. The 200 call is trading at 23p and the 220 at 10p. At this point he judges it worthwhile closing the strategy. With a further eleven weeks to run to expiry, there should still be some positive time value present in the strategy to be recouped.

PROFIT/LOSS: the profit on the strategy is equal to the 13p net premium on the position less the net cost of the strategy (8p). The overall profit is therefore 5p per share or £250. The outlay of £400 has produced a profit of £250 over two months. Immediately prior to expiry, the profit on the strategy would simply have been the difference between the strategy's net cost and the intrinsic value of the bought call.

SOME OTHER POSSIBLE OUTCOMES: *the shares rise only slightly over the two months following the initiation of the trade and stand at 208p.* The investor is faced with a choice of continuing to maintain the strategy until expiry in the hope that a further rise in price will leave it in profit, or closing the position and suffering no loss.

Rather than rise in price the shares fall back to below 200p. At expiry this would result in the whole of the capital committed to the trade being lost. Prior to expiry it may be possible for the investor to recoup the residual net time value (probably minimal) in the position.

CHART: *Chart 13* on page 134 shows the profit profile of the bull call spread at expiry and at different share prices.

ICHS Investments Option Strategy

Buy 1 July 200 call @ 16p. Write 1 July 220 Call @ 8p. 'Bull Call Spread'.

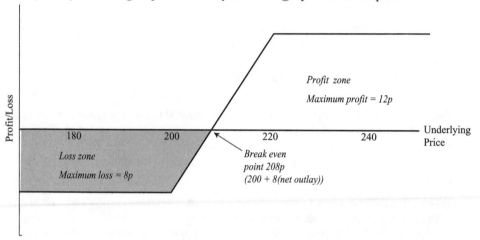

Chart 13: ICHS Investments - Bull Call Spread.

The horizontal lines on the chart represent the points of maximum profit and maximum loss determined by respectively the strike prices of the two calls and the net cost of the strategy.

It can probably be seen intuitively that an investor looking to speculate about a moderate fall in the price of an underlying share can give effect to this view by still using call options but in this case by writing the call with the lower strike price and buying the call with the higher strike price.

Because the call with the lower strike price is being written, the establishment of a strategy of this type will normally result in the investor receiving a net credit. However, since the series held has the higher strike price, and is therefore partly uncovered, the transaction is margined.

This is known as a **bear call spread** and is illustrated in the following example.

Example 10:

A moderately bearish view - A BEAR CALL SPREAD.

VIEW: on 1st October the investor takes the view that the shares in Southview Sunshades plc look a little overvalued. There are no announcements due for several months, the stockmarket looks modestly overvalued and, given the company's seasonal bias, no excitement in the shares is expected until the spring. The shares stand at 228p.

ACTION: establish a bear call spread. Buy 5 Southview January 240 calls at 9p and write 5 January 220 calls at 20p. This gives the investor a net credit of 11p per contract or £550 for the strategy. In this instance the maximum profit potential is the credit received at the outset, achieved if the shares fall to 220p or below. The break even point on the strategy is achieved at the lower exercise price plus the credit on the strategy. In this instance the break even point is therefore 231p. The maximum loss is the spread less the cost of the strategy, in other words 20p minus 11p (ie. 9p). This would be sustained in the event that the shares rise rather than fall and at expiry are at 240p or higher. It can be seen that this profit profile is the reverse image of that outlined above for *Example 9* on page 133.

WHAT HAPPENS NEXT: the shares do indeed fall steadily between October and January and at expiry stand at 215p. The profit on the strategy remains the credit received at the outset since both options are worthless at this point. The investor has therefore made £550.

SOME OTHER POSSIBLE OUTCOMES: *instead of falling the shares rise and on expiry stand at 255p.* The positions are closed immediately prior to expiry. The price of both options at this point is equivalent to their intrinsic value. Closing the transaction means that in theory the 220 calls are bought back at 35p and the 240 calls sold at 15p. The net liability on closing the five contracts is therefore 20p per contract or £1,000 for the strategy which, when offset against the credit originally received, gives a net loss overall of £450.

The shares are unchanged on expiry and stand at 228p. The bought call has no value but the written call can in theory be bought back at 8p leaving the overall profit on the transaction at 3p (the original 11p credit minus the 8p cost of closing), a profit for the five-contract strategy of some £180.

CHART: the chart at expiry of the net position established by the bear call spread is shown on page 136. As can be seen this is the reverse of the previous chart.

There is a drawback to this strategy, however. Whereas in the case of a bull

Southview Sunshades Option Strategy

Buy 1 January 240 call @ 9p. Write 1 January 220 Call @ 20p. 'Bear Call Spread'.

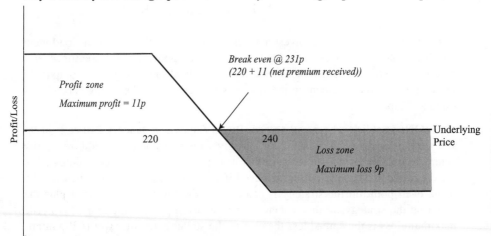

Chart 14: Southview Sunshades - Bear Call Spread.

call spread the position can be established at a lower cost than a straight option purchase and therefore breaks even more quickly, in the case of the bear call spread the maximum profit possible is received via the net credit at the outset. The problem is that the strategy may not come to fruition.

An option writer has no control over whether or not (or when) the holder of the option on the other side of the transaction will decide to exercise. If the written side of the strategy is therefore in-the-money, as it is in the case of the example above, there is an ever-present risk that the strategy will collapse because of early exercise. This risk, and the fact that margin is required, represent the main disadvantages of the strategy.

It can probably be seen from these examples and those in preceding chapters that it is possible to tailor spreads, by using different combinations of strike prices relative to the price of the underlying shares, to cater for differing degrees of bullishness and bearishness. In the case of the bull call spread, for instance, the further out-of-the-money the spread created the more bullish the investor would be. The cost of implementing the strategy would be lower, and therefore the potential profit (that is the spread less the cost of the strategy) would be larger. The shares would, however, have to rise further before the strategy was in a profit-making position.

Looking back at Example 9, for instance, if the 220 calls were bought at 8p and, say, the 240 calls written at 4p, the maximum profit potential for an outlay of 4p per contract would be 16p, a 4:1 ratio rather than the near 1:1 profit:outlay ratio in the original scenario. The only stipulation is the share price would have to rise from the original 204p to 224p before the strategy would break even.

Spreads using put options can be set up in the same way. As may already have been deduced, the bull put spread is equivalent in terms of profit profile to a bull call spread (the former being the purchase of a put at one exercise price and the writing of a put at a higher exercise price). Similarly a bear put spread, where a put with one exercise price is bought and a put with a lower exercise price written, is similar to a bear call spread in terms of its profit profile.

The choice of one over the other will depend on their relative break even points and whether or not the investor is prepared to put up margin. Margin is required in the case of the bear call spread and the bull put spread. Whatever spread is chosen, the profit potential is either the credit received at the outset, or, in the case of a strategy which results in a net initial debit, the spread (that is, the difference between the exercise prices of the two options involved) minus the initial debit.

For obvious reasons, these four types of strategy outlined above are known as vertical spreads, since they seek to take advantage of upward and downward movements in the underlying share price.

Calendar Spreads

Just as there are vertical spreads, however, so there are horizontal ones too. These are more normally known as calendar (or time) spreads and are based on the principle that time decay in longer-dated options is slower than in options where expiry is closer.

This type of strategy is essentially a simple one. The options involved have the same strike price, the nearer expiry month is written and further expiry month is bought.

There are a number of facets to this strategy. The first is that, if it is felt that the shares may move up (or down, in the case of a put) in price, but not for a little while, then structuring the deal as a calendar spread means that the cost of what will eventually (once the near month has expired) become a normal option position is reduced by the amount of the premium received for writing the near month option.

However, prior to the expiry of the near month option, the profit potential of the strategy is limited. Another disadvantage of these strategies is that, if the original judgement proves incorrect and the shares begin to move sharply in price as soon as the strategy is implemented, the whole plan can be disrupted by early exercise of the written option.

This is outlined in the example below:

Example 11:

A delayed bullish view - A CALENDAR SPREAD

VIEW: Fertile Fast Foods plc stands at 288p on 1st August. The October 280 calls are 24p and the January 280 calls are 30p. You believe that the October calls look a little overpriced and that nothing is likely to happen to the price until around the turn of the year when the results will be announced and after which the shares should rise.

ACTION: write 5 October 280 calls and buy five January 280 calls. The total cost of the strategy is a net 6p, or £300 for the five contracts.

WHAT HAPPENS NEXT: at the end of October the shares stand at 278p and the written October 280 calls expire worthless. The position then becomes a straight long position in five contracts of the January 280 calls. Any rise in price above the 286p mark will result in a profit. The results are announced in December and the shares rise to 320p.

PROFIT/LOSS: on expiry the options have an intrinsic value of 40p, realising £2,000 for the strategy and giving, once the initial cost of the strategy is deducted, a net profit of £1,700 for an outlay of £300 and an 11% rise in the underlying share price over the period.

SOME OTHER POSSIBLE OUTCOMES: *the shares become subject to takeover rumours and rise to 300p almost immediately the strategy is implemented.* The written option is exercised and, in order to be able to deliver the stock, the longer-dated bought option is in turn exercised by the investor. The prices of the two options rise to 36p and 42p respectively: each now has 20p of intrinsic value and the same time value as before. This result is that the position has effectively been reversed for the same net difference and no profit or loss results.

The shares fall to 260p and remain there until after the expiry of the longer-dated option. Both options in turn expire worthless. Once the near month has expired the investor may or may not take the view that a price recovery is unlikely in the remaining option. If it is thought that the situation has changed fundamentally, the other option can be sold to recoup the remaining time value in the option. This may or may not be greater than the initial debit incurred from implementing the strategy in the first place.

CHART: the chart of the strategy immediately prior to the expiry of the October option is shown below.

Prior to this expiry if the shares rise above the 280p mark, and assuming no exercise takes place, the spread between the two options widens. This can be seen from the downward slope in the profit line from 280p upwards.

As with vertical spreads, the same profit profile can be achieved whether or not the options are calls or puts. Similarly, the longer-dated calls can be written and the shorter ones bought to create what is known as a reverse calendar spread. In this instance the risks and rewards are the reverse of the example above, with a credit being received at the outset. The common features of all calendar spreads are that profit and losses are limited prior to the near month expiry and that the position can be disrupted by early exercise of the written option.

Fertile Fast Foods Option Strategy

Write 1 October 280 call @ 24p. Buy 1 January 280 Call @ 30p. 'Calendar Spread'.

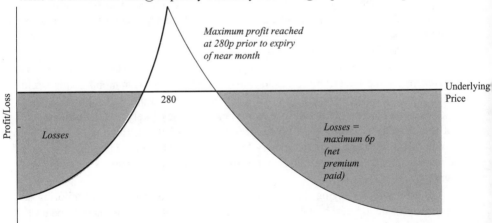

Chart 15: Fertile Fast Foods - A Calendar Spread.

Diagonal Spreads

It is probably obvious from the above that there is no need for the investor to confine himself necessarily to the rules outlined above for establishing spread strategies. For each option stock standing at a particular price there are a sizeable number of combinations of spread strategies that can be implemented.

A typical option stock, for instance, depending on the degree to which it has fluctuated in the past, might have six separate call option series in each expiry month making a total of 18 series in all. In theory any one of these can be combined in a spread strategy with any other. Which series are chosen will depend on the view being taken of the market and the outlook for that particular stock, and indeed where the price of the shares stands at that point in time.

A further variant of spread strategies therefore is the diagonal spread. This is essentially a cross between a horizontal and a vertical spread. One side of the strategy involves writing an option with a particular expiry date and strike price. Unlike either a vertical or horizontal spread, the other side of a diagonal spread strategy involves the purchase of an option where both the strike price and the expiry month are different.

However, the normal expression of this strategy is the writing of a near month call (or put) and the purchase of a longer-dated and further out-of-the-money call (or put). Since the longer-dated of the two options will have higher time value, it is possible that the diagonal spread can be achieved for very low cost, or even a net credit.

Once again the attraction of the strategy is that it enables the investor to get into the longer-dated call at a very low price or even a credit. The ideal scenario is therefore for the underlying price to move little until the near month expires and then for it to rally strongly. As with the previous examples of spreads, early exercise can be a problem and if exercise begins to look likely and the written side of the strategy is closed as a precaution, the cost of doing this may exceed the value of the further out-of-the-money long position. Margin is also required for a diagonal spread since in certain circumstances the position resembles an uncovered write.

It goes without saying that such positions need extremely close monitoring so that evasive action can be taken if an undesirable set of circumstances appears to be materialising.

Butterfly Spreads

Just as individual options can be combined in the form of spread strategies, so two spreads can be combined in more complex formulations. One of the most common is the combination of a bull and bear spread with a common middle exercise price.

The effect of this, in the case of a call option strategy, for instance would be to buy an in-the-money call, to write two at-the-money or near-the-money calls and to buy an out-of-the money call - all with the same expiry date.

This technique is probably best explained by an example.

Example 12:

A BUTTERFLY SPREAD

VIEW: it is 1st January. Lepidopter Holdings stands at 270p and an investor believes that its share price is unlikely to move much for the next few months. If anything it may rise slightly. This neutral-to-bullish stance calls for the establishment of a butterfly spread strategy, which leaves a low chance of losing money and offers a reasonable chance of profiting if there is little movement in the shares.

ACTION: buy 5 April 260 calls at 23p, write 10 April 280 calls at 14p, and buy 5 April 300 calls at 7p. The net cost of the strategy is a net debit of 2p on 5 contracts, or £100. This is calculated by adding together the cost of the bought calls and deducting the revenue received from the written calls. Although there are ten written calls, in effect the transaction is two adjoining spreads of five contracts. The 2p net cost of the strategy represents the maximum loss on the strategy. Profits will accrue in this instance between 298p and 262p, the upper and lower exercise prices respectively adjusted to allow for the net cost of the strategy. Maximum profits are generated if, at expiry, the underlying share price stands at the middle exercise price of 280p, In this instance the profit is equivalent to 18p, one of the spreads (20p) minus the cost of the strategy (2p).

WHAT HAPPENS NEXT: the investor has been wrong about the shares and they rise to 290p just prior to expiry. The strategy is still in profit, but the best expectations have not been borne out. The intrinsic value of the 260 calls is now 30p and that of the 280 calls 10p. The 300 calls have no value.

PROFIT/LOSS: assuming the option position is closed in the market rather than through exercise the cash received from the sale of the five 260 calls, £1,500, will be offset by the cost of closing the write of the 10 280 calls, £1,000, leaving net revenue of £500. Deducting the original cost of the strategy leaves a net profit of £400.

SOME OTHER POSSIBLE OUTCOMES: *the company issues a profits warning and the shares fall back to 230p.* The entire position expires worthless and the loss

141

is limited to the net 2p cost of establishing the position, that is £100 for the five contracts involved.

The shares gradually drift up to expire at 280p. The ideal circumstance. It is not worth the holders of the written calls exercising their options, and although the 300 call is worthless there is a profit of 20p on the 260 calls. The total profit on the strategy is therefore the gain on the 260 calls, £1,000 for the five contracts, less the £100 cost of establishing the strategy, ie. £900.

CHART: the profit profile of this strategy at expiry is shown in *Chart 16* below.

It is probably best to see such a strategy as the combination of two separate spreads, a bull call spread (the purchase of the 260 and sale of the 280) and a bear call spread (the purchase of the 300 and the sale of the 280). Butterfly strategies more often than not come into being in this way, rather than being planned at the outset. This could occur either through setting up a complementary spread trade next to an existing one, or else through some other combination of deals.

Lepidopter Holdings Option Strategy
Buy 1 April 260 call @ 23p. Write 2 April 280 Calls @ 14p.
Buy 1 April 300 Call @ 7p. 'Butterfly spread'

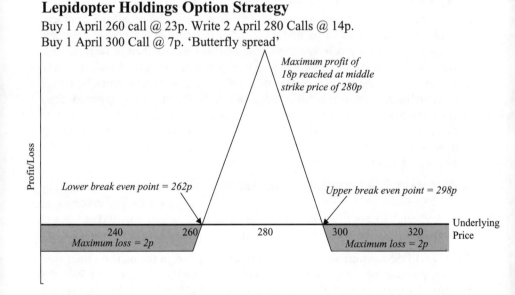

Chart 16: Lepidopter Holdings - A Butterfly Spread.

As with other spread strategies, though there is a limited loss potential, there is also a limited profit potential. Since one part of the strategy is in effect an uncovered sale, the whole strategy must be margined and, as with other spreads, there is the risk that the position can be disrupted by the early exercise of the written side.

A further caveat can also be added. This is that in practice, because the strategy involves multiple legs and different numbers of contracts, the likelihood is that dealing costs will have a depressing effect on the profit potential of the strategy. These have been ignored in the example above.

Ratio Spreads

In all of the above examples, it has been assumed that the same numbers of contracts are involved on each side of an options strategy. However, this need not be so. Spreads can be constructed where, because of the difference in prices of the individual options, a strategy can be put in place where an uneven number of options may be involved at no net cost.

For instance, imagine that an option stock has July 200 calls priced at 16p and July 220 calls priced at 8p, with the price of the shares at, say, 204p. It can easily be seen that a spread can be constructed at no net cost (excluding dealing expenses) which involves buying and writing the two different calls in the ratio of 1:2. In this instance, buying one 200 call and writing two 220 calls gives a maximum profit if the position is closed just prior to expiry with the shares at 220p, but the possibility of unlimited loss if they rise above 240p.

Ratio Spread

Buy 1 July 200 call @ 16p. Write 2 July 220 Calls @ 8p

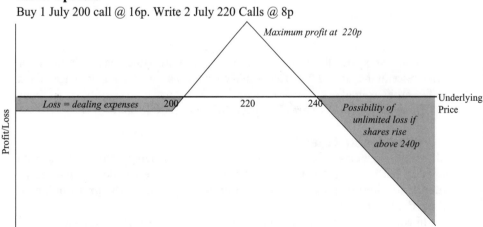

Chart 17: Ratio Spread.

Ratio Backspread
Write 1 July 200 Call @ 16p. Buy 2 July 220 Calls @ 8p

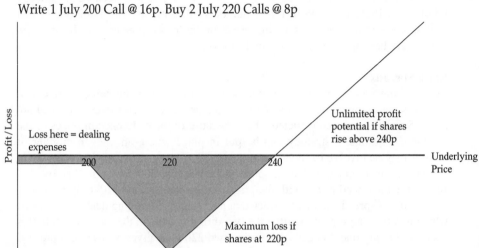

Chart 18: Ratio Backspread.

The reverse position (known as a **backspread**) would in this instance involve buying the calls with the higher strike price and writing the ones with the lower strike price in the ratio of 2:1. This would create a chart with a mirror image to that of the earlier example.

These are shown in *Chart 17* on page 143 and *Chart 18* above.

Using Complex Strategies
All of the strategies described above are capable of being used by the private investor, but it should be stressed that they require close monitoring. **Particular attention should be paid to the impact of dealing costs on the profit potential of particular strategies.**

In addition it is strongly recommended that investors seek to become familiar with simple option strategies and the way they behave before attempting some of these more complex variations.

It is also worthwhile being aware that the strategies outlined above are only a handful of the variations available in the option market.

Investors should ensure that they become well aware of the characteristics, potential profitability and loss parameters of these complex trades before entering into them, and of the dealing costs involved. Rehearsing the profit/loss characteristics of these strategies on a computer model is advisable prior to dealing.

Summary

1. More complex options strategies normally involve buying one option and writing a different one. In some cases these strategies are subject to margin requirements and this, and dealing costs, should always be factored in when looking at their profit or loss potential.

2. Spreads (or vertical spreads) involve the buying of one option and the writing (selling) of another with the same expiry date but with a higher or lower strike price. In a bull spread the written option has the higher strike price; in a bear spread the written option has the lower strike price. The degree of bullishness or bearishness involved can be tailored through the choice of exercise price.

3. Calendar spreads involve the same principle, but are where the strike price of the two options is the same, but the expiry date is different. These strategies look to profit from the different rate of time decay between the two options. Normally the written option is the earlier to expire of the two. After expiry of the near month, the position becomes a straightforward single option holding. Calendar spreads can be used to give effect to a view which is bullish or bearish, but with a time delay. Until expiry of the near month, profit potential is limited.

4. One drawback common to both vertical and calendar spreads is that, if the price moves sharply sooner than anticipated, the strategy runs the risk of early exercise of the written option and may suffer extra costs as a result of the consequent closing of the other side of the strategy. Against this, the cost of spread strategy is modest, because the cost of the bought option is wholly or partly offset by the premium received from the written side of the strategy.

5. Diagonal spreads involve the same principle, but occur where both expiry month and strike price are different. Ratio spreads involve combining a different number of contracts on one side of the strategy (ie. buying one contract but writing two, lower priced, contracts, or vice versa).

6. A butterfly spread is the simultaneous combination of a bull spread and a bear spread, normally with a common middle exercise price which represents the point of maximum profit on expiry.

7. Common features of all these strategies, and other more complex ones not mentioned, are low cost, limited profit potential, higher dealing costs, the possibility of margin, but the opportunity to profit from comparatively small movements in the underlying shares.

TEN

USING SHARE PRICE CHARTS FOR OPTION TIMING

Earlier chapters of this book have dealt almost exclusively with the option market and concepts related to it. But all this is not much use without some innate understanding about how the price of an underlying security is likely to behave.

Looking at the fundamentals of a company's business can help, but it is only part of the story. This division between analysing a company's business and attempting to predict its share price from past trends has long been a source of debate in the investment world.

Analysts generally divide neatly into two camps: fundamental analysts and technical analysts.

Fundamental analysts look at balance sheets, profit records, and the background to the industry in which a company operates, to arrive at a conclusion about whether a particular share is cheap or dear.

Technical analysts maintain that this is a waste of time, and that all this information is already distilled into the price of the shares. They argue that what is much more important is studying how share prices have behaved in different market circumstances in the past, and how buyers and sellers have reacted at different price levels. Studying these patterns can, it is claimed, help assess how prices will behave in the future.

Fundamental analysts and technical analysts each tend to be critical of the other; in reality the astute investor needs to learn to use both techniques. They are complementary in a number of respects. From a long term investment standpoint, fundamental analysis may be of more use, but technical analysis cannot be ignored for the shorter term timing of purchases and sales.

It is impossible in the space of one chapter of this book to cover technical analysis comprehensively. The reader is therefore advised to consult the books mentioned here and in the appendix for a more detailed explanation of the techniques involved.

It is more convenient to use the techniques described below using a computer-based technical analysis charting package. These were mentioned in passing in Chapter Eight. Assuming the investor has a PC, acquiring the relevant software is relatively inexpensive. Good packages are available for under £100 with data charges of around £10 per month for a dial-up database or with data delivered free by email for those with an Internet connection.

In some cases manuals accompanying such software will have brief explanations of the way different technical indicators are calculated and the use to which they can be put. Alternatively, a basic guide to the subject can be used.

A large part of technical analysis is concerned with the statistical analysis of share price movements, and has in this respect some similarities with the statistical concept of volatility explained earlier in this book. As was noted there, volatility is vital to analysing and pricing options. And certain other statistical aspects of technical analysis lend themselves to analysing the movements in the underlying securities, with particular reference to trading in options.

Trends, Support and Resistance

One of the reasons why technical analysis is a valid tool for investors to use is that it reflects the behaviour of investors. First, it can point to the way investors have behaved in the past (by indicating levels at which they have bought a particular share heavily and levels at which they may have sold). But it also works to some degree because the market believes it will. Investors in the market follow share prices and, either scientifically or intuitively, tend to respond in the same consistent way to known technical indicators which reflect past behaviour.

An established investment principle is that 'the trend is your friend'. In other words, a trend will continue until a specific event occurs to reverse it. No share price moves up or down in a straight line, but fluctuations within a narrow or wider band may gradually take a share price higher or lower. In simple terms, once these trends are established, prices tend to bounce up off the lower limit of a particular trend line and down off the upper limit.

This is shown in the chart of British Steel. As can be seen, from the start of 1993 through to the end of 1994 its share price rose in a sharp uptrend from a low of 43p to around 175p, with each new peak and each successive trough being higher than the previous one. Drawing lines on the chart roughly connecting these points can be seen in the centre of the chart.

Chart 19: British Steel.

In the course of 1995 the pattern became less clear, with the trend first being broken and then continuing for a spell, while subsequently the shares have fluctuated between 150p and 200p.

Equally important, especially in the case of shares which have established no definable trend, or after a trend is broken, is the concept of support and resistance.

Support levels are points at which, in the past, buying interest has tended to emerge, thus 'supporting' the price. The assumption is that if buying interest has been established at a particular price level, it is likely to recur if that price point is hit again in the future. Similarly if, after a significant appreciation in its price, a share meets selling pressure at a particular price level, it will struggle to rise above it. This is known as a resistance level. Repeated failures to break through resistance levels may be a prelude to a more severe downturn.

Both support and resistance levels can also be seen on the chart, as indicated by the two horizontal lines to the right and the left of the trend 'tramlines'. Between 1989 and 1991, British Steel repeatedly failed to break through the resistance level at 150p and subsequently fell sharply.

As previously mentioned, support and resistance work because they are perceived to have an influence over investor behaviour. But support and resistance levels and, for that matter trend lines, are made to be broken. And another of their features is that, once they have been convincingly broken, a support level subsequently becomes a resistance level and vice versa.

Again, this can be seen in the case of British Steel. Once the uptrend had carried the shares back up through the previous 150p resistance level, the shares have repeatedly dropped back down to this level and then found support.

There is a reason for this, which goes back to investor psychology. Resistance works because earlier buyers of the shares who have seen a subsequent fall in price want to get back out when the price moves back up to their original buying level, rather than take a loss. This is human nature, although not necessarily good investment discipline. Equally, support levels crop up if earlier potential buyers have been frustrated because the price appreciated before they had chance to put the order on. They will be keen to buy if the share price drops back to the earlier level, especially if past evidence suggests it is an area where other investors may be tempted to buy, too.

Concepts like this are vitally important to an understanding of how share prices move. Before contemplating an option trade be realistic about where the share price could go, and where potential buyers and sellers might come in. Trading in the related options without appreciating the technical position in the underlying shares is the same as driving a car with one's eyes tightly shut, with a similar likelihood of dire consequences.

It is a good principle of technical analysis, however, not to rely solely on one indicator to generate a buying or selling decision. One way of confirming a change in direction, or for that matter a convincing break through a previously long-established trend, is an increase in the volume of shares traded. These are published, for the major stocks, each day in the *Financial Times*. Changes in volume should be monitored closely. A break-out from a previously well-defined trend on low volume is likely to lack follow-through, while one accompanied by heavy volume is more likely to indicate that a lasting change has occurred.

Another interesting way of looking at trends in share prices and implications for options prices is through regression analysis and confidence intervals. This involves taking the underlying data and charting a 'line of best fit' which minimises the sum of the distance of each of the points from the line. This is actually known as 'least squares' regression in statistics-speak because the formula for calculating it actually takes as its basis the squares of the variation of each point from the average. Once again, computers take the donkey-work out of doing the calculation.

A by-product of the analysis is a measure called the 'standard deviation'. In simple terms, this is the average distance from the line of best fit. It can be statistically proved that lines drawn one standard deviation either side of the line of best fit will contain the swings in the underlying data roughly two-thirds of the time. Similarly, two standard deviations should contain 95% of the data. The chart shows the course of Norwich Union's share price between June and December 1997. The middle of the three lines superimposed on the chart is the line of best fit, while the two lines either side are one standard deviation either side of it.

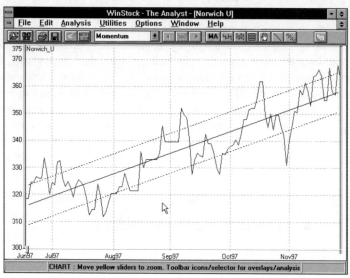

Chart 20: Norwich Union 'line of best fit' and confidence limits..

The interesting point about all this is that standard deviation is a very good indication of volatility.

Moving Averages and Related Indicators
It almost goes without saying that share prices often move around by small amounts, and sometimes by larger ones, on a day-to-day basis. These movements reflect the conflicting pull of buyers and sellers in the market, news events, the overall market background and various other extraneous factors. Calculating a moving average eliminates this 'interference' factor, or 'static', in the share price trend by smoothing the patterns out over a period of days, enabling one to discern a clearer picture.

How are these averages calculated? The concept is a straightforward one. A 20-day moving average, for instance, adds together the price of a share at the close on each of the previous 20 days and divides by 20. The following day, the latest closing price is added and the oldest price of the previous series is dropped off and the resulting total divided by 20 to arrive at the next 'observation'. Once a series has been built up, it can be graphed in the normal way.

This is a laborious method of charting, and one which technical analysts used to do by hand. Fortunately, the method lends itself to computerised number-crunching. Moving averages can be calculated over any period of days. The shorter the period, the closer will the average resemble the underlying data, and the longer the period, the smoother the underlying trend will appear.

It has been observed over the years by technical analysts that moving averages of different lengths have distinct relationships with each other and with the underlying data from which they are calculated. A shorter-term average crossing a longer-term average, especially when both are moving in the same direction, for instance, can be a good indication that a longer-term trendline has been broken.

In some instances too, the trend in the underlying price relative to a moving average can be of significance. A price moving up through a longer term moving average is held to be bullish, and one moving down through a longer term uptrend can be taken as a sell signal.

Chart 21: Ladbroke Group - Moving Averages.

Looking at the interaction of two moving averages, the chart shows the 35 and 90 day moving averages for Ladbroke Group, together with the underlying price of the shares. It can be seen that the shorter average swings around in a more pronounced way than the longer average and crosses it at certain points. Observation suggests that these crossover points correspond broadly to the turning points in the underlying price.

The emphasis is on the word 'broadly'. For example, in January 1994 the 35-day average moved up through the 90-day average, generating a buying signal. This coincided with a sharp upward move in the price, but it would have been impossible for an investor, had he or she waited for the signal, to have caught the move in time. Indicators generated by moving averages tend to be trend-following, rather than predictors of trend changes. Moving averages may provide a useful function in confirming a change in trend but, for the purposes of trading in options, they have their limitations.

A more fruitful approach is to take the data provided by moving averages and use it in a different way. For instance, a simple chart of the difference between the value of two moving averages might be a better indicator, in that it will show a possible turning point earlier as the two averages begin to come together.

A good way of looking at this is what is known as a moving average convergence or divergence (or MACD) line. This takes the differences between two averages, but smooths out the kinks in the line to eliminate 'false alarms'. Sometimes two lines are plotted, arrived at through using different smoothing factors. In this instance, one line acts as the trend and the other as the trigger, with the buy signal generated when the trigger crosses the line when the value is below zero and the sell signal created when the trigger moves down through the line when it is above zero. However, even a simple MACD is a good indicator of turning points, as shown in the chart.

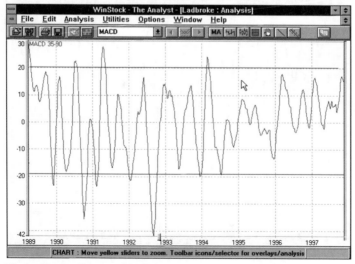

Chart 22: Ladbroke Group - MACD.

It can be seen that the indicator works best when the divergence is at its most extreme. This can be judged by looking back at the previous price history. In the case of Ladbroke, for example, it is possible that an investor could have captured some of the big moves in the underlying share price, for instance those between September 1992 and February 1993 and those between December 1993 and February 1994. But it is a matter of judgement how tightly one would want to set the parameters in contemplating trades. Indicators like this are not infallible, and trading too frequently can simply result in over heavy dealing costs and low profits.

Extreme movements (such as those in mid-1990, early 1991, autumn 1992 and early 1994) give the biggest indicator of a subsequent reversal which could be exploited via the option market. One caveat here, of course, is that extreme movements of this type in a share price, may also be accompanied by a rise in volatility, and hence option premiums.

Another oscillator of this type is the overbought/oversold indicator (OBOS). This measures the difference between the price of the security itself and a selected moving average. The choice of moving average period is important in this context. The choice of a very short period will produce a line with a lot of swings and less predictive value, while a long period will tend to resemble the price of the underlying shares themselves. The OBOS for Ladbroke, for instance, on the basis of a 50-day moving average is shown in the chart.

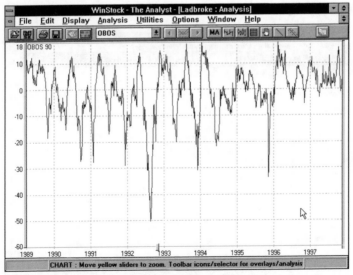

Chart 23: Ladbroke Group - Overbought/Oversold Indicator.

What would be sought here from the standpoint of a possible option trade is a change in direction from deep in either overbought or oversold territory. The likely size of the price move could be determined by looking at likely support and resistance levels and structuring a strategy accordingly. The definition of what constitutes overbought or oversold differs depending on which average is chosen and from stock to stock. In Ladbroke's case, oversold territory seems to be the -20% range, while the shares look overbought if the indicator is in the 12-15% range.

One should, however, beware of relying too slavishly on these indicators. Moving averages, and the indicators based on them, can and do converge and diverge simply through a gradual accumulation of small movements in the underlying shares - a big adjustment is not guaranteed.

Secondly, allowance must be made for the time which these moves may take to come to fruition. This may be longer than the life of a single option. In addition, option writers and market makers clearly have access to the same information as a potential option investor and option premiums may well adjust accordingly. Finally, the bid-offer spread and dealing costs must be taken into account.

Momentum and Related Indicators

A different way of looking at trends in share prices, and one which can be particularly useful for option trading, is to examine share price momentum.

Momentum indicators measure the increasing or decreasing rate of change of individual share prices. They work on the principle that momentum is highest early in a trend and then steadily decreases. The best analogy for this is that of a ball thrown into the air. First the rise is rapid, but its upward momentum declines as gravity reasserts itself and then it begins to fall, slowly at first and then with increasing velocity.

Momentum indicators can be used to spot turning points. A normal momentum chart plots the smoothed moving change (plus or minus) in a share price over the chosen period of days, with the resulting figures calculated as a percentage. Looking once again at Ladbroke, the 35-day momentum chart will appear like Chart 24 overleaf. This seems to indicate that changes greater and plus or minus 20% are significant indicators, although the chart should be compared with the underlying price changes to see how this could be used in terms of trading the shares or the options.

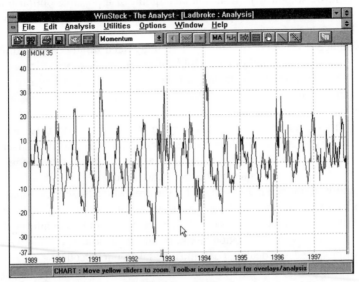

Chart 24: Ladbroke Group - 35-day Momentum.

A simpler indicator is known as the Meisels index, developed by a Canadian stockbroker, Ron Meisels. It merely involves counting how many days a share price has risen, and how many days it has fallen over, say, a moving ten-day period. The number of falls is subtracted from the number of rises and the result plotted on a chart. If a ten-day period is chosen, the maximum value on the chart will be +10 (when the share price rises ten days in a row) and the minimum -10. Anything over +6 would in this context be considered overbought, and anything under -6 would be considered oversold. If a longer Meisels period (say 50 days) is chosen, the likelihood is that the significant indicator would be a proportionately smaller number. In other words, if a ten day period were chosen, it is just about possible for a share to rise each of ten successive days. In any period of 50 days, the maximum number of consecutive daily rises might only be, say, 20. The significant level is normally obvious from observation of the chart. The other point is that a long-term Meisels chart is likely to look pretty confusing, so a time period of, say, six or 12 months may be a better one to use than one of six or 12 years. The chart shows the 10-day Meisels chart for Ladbroke over a 12-month period.

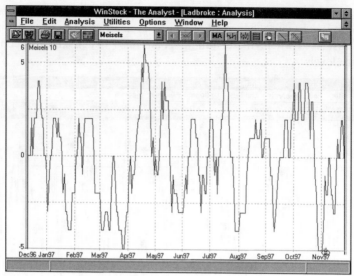

Chart 25: Ladbroke Group - Meisels Indicator Chart.

This produces two instances of an overbought share price and two instances of an oversold one in the space of a 12-month period. From a trading standpoint, however, only one instance, the move down from a level of 275p to 242p in July/August, might conceivably have been profitable from the standpoint of an option transaction. Meisels is arguably best used as a way of confirming an opportunity flagged by other indicators.

A more complex variation of this indicator is the Rate of Change Index, sometimes also known as the Welles-Wilder Relative Strength Index (RSI), after its inventor. Here the principle is the same as the Meisels Index, except that instead of the number of days, the changes in the price on the 'up' days are added together and subtracted from the aggregate changes on the 'down' days to arrive at the index. A 14 or 20 day period is typically chosen and the index plotted as a percentage. A move over 70 is generally considered as overbought, and under 30 oversold. The general tendency is for the index to peak or trough just before the price history itself. This can be verified by comparing the two charts. For Ladbroke, the 20-day RSI figure looks like this with the 70 and 30 levels indicated by the horizontal lines. Again, the choice of a relatively short time period helps to eliminate confusion.

Here again, the indicator would have caught one or two potentially profitable moves in the underlying share price. The important point, however, is

157

not just to find stocks whose RSI is over 70 or under 30, but those where it is at these points but has just changed direction. It is clearly also important if possible to find instances where these turning points also match known support and resistance levels.

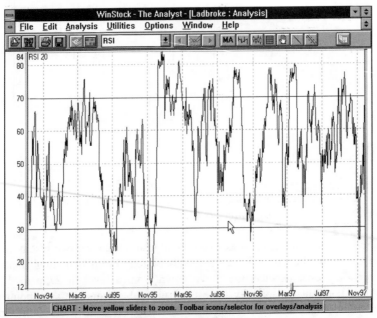

Chart 26: Ladbroke Group - 20-day RSI Figure.

Also in the technical analyst's repertoire are what are known as stochastic indicators (or simply stochastics). These can be of use in certain circumstances. They tend to be more effective in establishing turning points in shares which show strong cyclical tendencies.

The stochastic value is calculated by taking the difference between today's price and the low point for the period being considered, compared with the difference between the highest and lowest price for the same period. It can, therefore, vary between zero and 100, the 100 point being reached when today's price is the highest price for the period under consideration, and zero being when it is at the lowest point. A simple stochastic of Ladbroke over a 15-day period would look as follows:

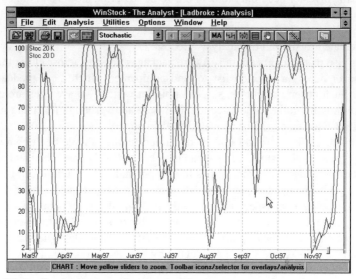

Chart 27: Ladbroke Group - Stochastic Chart.

Rather like the analysis of moving averages outlined earlier, stochastics are of particular significance where divergence occurs in what appear to be major overbought or oversold areas. This might occur, for instance, when the share price rises to a new high, but the stochastic fails to rise in sympathy. This would be taken as a sell signal. Similarly, when the price falls to a new low but the stochastic doesn't, this could be taken as an imminent buying opportunity. In each instance, the pending change could perhaps form the subject of a particular option strategy.

Once again, as with moving averages, smoothed values can be used to produce a 'trigger' effect.

How to Use these Indicators

It is obvious, from the complexity of the calculations required to compile these indicators, that a computerised technical analysis package is the only way to perform analyses of this sort.

Even then, with the data which many of these systems are capable of storing, the investor is still faced with a daunting task of sifting through hundreds of charts to find option stocks which fit the desired pattern.

Fortunately, it is possible to simplify this task somewhat. In the first place, for the purpose of highlighting opportunities which might arise in the equity options market, the investor need only look at the 70 or so option stocks and the FTSE 100 Index itself.

Most chart analysis packages contain a facility whereby a selected list of stocks can be created to shorten the analysis process.

It is also possible, in certain software packages, to scan across either the whole database or across a selected list to find companies which meet predetermined criteria. Such criteria might be, say, the point at which two averages are crossing and both moving in the same direction, or where an overbought/oversold indicator has just reversed below 30 or above 70, and so on.

If this discipline is followed each day, opportunities should be thrown up from time to time in option stocks. These can then be studied further. The ideal situation would be one where the technical position of one indicator is reinforced by several others to give a composite picture of whether a stock is cheap or expensive.

This is only one aspect of the analysis from the standpoint of the option investor, however. What is, of course, required is not just a likely movement in the shares, but one which takes place within a specified timescale. Whether or not this is probable can be deduced to some degree by observation of the price chart.

Then the option chosen should be one which leaves ample time for the expected move to take place on the basis of what has happened in the past. In the case of Ladbroke, for instance, as shown in the line chart, its moves between the extremes of the recent trading range have typically taken as much as four months to complete.

It should also be stressed that the indicators outlined above are only illustrations of what can be derived from chart packages of this type. With experience, the investor may find other indices which it is felt intuitively offer a better way of predicting the timing and length of particular moves, or which are more relevant for selecting candidates for specific option trades.

It is also vital not to understate the importance of support and resistance levels. These are simple concepts easily observed from price charts published in magazines like the *Investors Chronicle* and in publications such as the *Estimate Directory* and *The Company Guide*. Up to a point, for those who watch particular share prices closely on a day-to-day basis, they are observable even without the benefit of a chart, simply by getting an empirical feel for the way prices react.

Two further points need to be stressed. One is that none of these indicators, or any others an investor might use, is infallible. Some work better with different stocks than others; some work well in certain market backgrounds and not in others; and the indicators may on occasion contradict each other. The investor may arrive at a good idea which seems right on the chart, only to find the price reacts before he or she has the chance to work out which individual option or option strategy might represent the best way of taking advantage of the situation.

One important final point is that the market (market-makers and other potential option buyers and sellers) must be assumed to be likely to have access to the same information. Making money as a result of purely studying charts is therefore difficult. The professionals' monitoring systems may be considerably more sophisticated than those likely to be used by the average private investor.

One way in which this is manifested will be in terms of options prices and implied volatility. In other words, if market-makers suspect that a technical situation is developing which could be favourable to option buyers, prices will be marked up accordingly so that writers are compensated for the additional risk involved.

The conclusion is that charts are best looked at in conjunction with fundamentals providing a composite picture of both the underlying company and its prospects, the technical position of the shares and their past history, and the best option strategies - buying or writing, spreads, straddles and so on - which might be appropriate, bearing in mind all of the relevant circumstances. Share price charts are an important part of the picture, but they are only one part.

As noted previously, there is extensive literature on the subject of charts and technical analysis, and certain books are worth studying in particular to gain an insight into how technical analysis can be applied.

A basic primer on the subject is Brian Millard's *Profitable Charting Techniques*, published by Qudos Publications, 16 Queensgate, Bramhall, Cheshire SK7 1JT. A more detailed exposition of the subject with specific application to derivatives is John Murphy's *Technical Analysis of the Futures Markets*, published by the New York Institute of Finance, 70 Pine Street, New York, NY10270. Despite its title, this is a comprehensive book on the application of technical analysis generally. It is full of market 'nous' accumulated by the author, a widely-respected market professional. Most chart software producers provide a basic explanation of the background to the calculation of technical indicators in their manuals.

Summary

1. A rudimentary knowledge of technical analysis (that is, the analysis of share price trends as opposed to company fundamentals) is important for successful options trading.

2. Low-cost software packages are available which will produce an array of technical indicators on a wide range of shares. Many of these easy-to-use packages have facilities which enable the scanning of a range of securities to see which, if any, conform to specific technical criteria.

3. The successful investor should be able to recognise and exploit support and resistance levels in charts of the shares which underlie particular options, and be able to recognise long-term trends.

4. Moving averages are useful for spotting changes in trends, but tend to produce reliable signals only after the event.

5. Moving average convergence and divergence indicators, such as 'gap' analysis and the MACD indicator, are more useful in this respect.

6. A variety of other indicators, ranging from the simple to the statistically sophisticated, can be used, basically to spot when shares are overbought and oversold and to recognise share price turning points.

7. The ideal situation is one where a particular conclusion can be drawn from several separate indicators, each of which reinforces the other. Trading volume can also be used as a confirmation factor.

8. Care must be taken to select the options concerned and structure a particular strategy so that there appears to be adequate time for it to come to fruition and that a profit can result after allowing for the impact of the bid-offer spread, erosion of time value, and dealing costs.

9. Technical analysis should not be used in isolation, but neither should it be ignored when determining the selection and timing of particular option strategies.

ELEVEN

OPTIONS ONLINE

Since the first edition of this book was published in 1995, there has been a substantial increase in both the numbers of computers in the UK that have an Internet connection, and in the number and variety of world wide web resources available to investors. Many of these are free and offer access to information hitherto only available to professional investors.

For those who have web access, or are considering getting connected in order to support their investing activities, this chapter is essential reading. Those who are not planning such a move can probably skip the next few pages.

For those in either category who want to read more on the subject of online investing there are a number of books that can help. My own book *The Online Investor* (John Wiley & Sons - 1997, 260pp £19.95) is a basic introduction to the subject of online investing, and how private investors can use the web to level an information playing field hitherto tilted very much in favour of the professional. Stephen Eckett's book *Investing Online*, (FT Pitman £39.95) is a weightier text on the subject and orientated to a greater degree towards the more professional, international reader. Due to be published by B. T. Batsford in November is *The Investors' Resource Book*, which will include full details of the top 50 investment books.

The web can help option investors in a number of ways, which are considered in turn later in this chapter.

Option traders frequently need access - as we have outlined earlier in this book - to fundamental information about companies in whose options they may wish to deal. This could include: general economic news that might affect the company concerned; information and news about specific companies, including profit announcements and other company information.

It also goes without saying that option prices and underlying price data and charting is useful to have. The role that charting underlying share prices can play in option trading is covered in a previous chapter, and some option traders (new to the game or more experienced) may already possess such software. Those who do not, though, may see the web as a convenient way of accessing this information.

Some option brokers have an online presence, and their sites can be a useful source of information about the market and about the viability of particular trading strategies. Likewise, many exchanges themselves, and LIFFE in particular (as far as the UK option investor is concerned), have sites which contain substantial quantities of useful information.

Finally, there is the question of how the web can be used as a source of software which would not otherwise be easily available to UK users and which can help investors with their trading. There are a number of free packages, mostly in the form of simple shareware programs and spreadsheet add-ins that, while not substituting for full-blown option valuation programs, can demonstrate the essentials of these programs and make it easier to select more sophisticated software at a later date.

One big advantage options have is that their language and the concepts and theory underlying them are universal. Hence many option pricing and valuation programs devised in the US can just as easily be used for valuing UK options.

On-line news

While many investors will tend to trade mainly in equity rather than index options, general economic news is an important commodity anyway. Leading shares move up and down to a greater or lesser degree in line with the market as a whole, and because option values can be sensitive to relatively small movements in price, trying to anticipate these movements is important to the average option trader.

Unfortunately, although the web can help, it's not quite as easy as that. Although there are sources of free news - organisations like Bloomberg and CNN, for example, have good web sites with a selection of up-to-date news headlines - access to real-time news as it happens tends to be more expensive. The cost has come down somewhat in recent years and organisations like ESI and Datastream/ICV, through its Market Eye web site, offer access to real-time news headlines for a subscription of a few pounds a month. Reuters is also moving into this market indirectly, via a service which is being marketed 'wholesale' via High Street banks and stockbrokers and which allows, for a modest monthly subscription, web access to economic and other company news through the bank or broker's own web site.

The problem is that most investors do not want to sit in front of their computer screens watching news headlines scroll up and down. Serious traders who want to do that will find that a subscription to a real time price and news feed from one of the several suppliers operating in this market will be a more worthwhile proposition. So the chance of anticipating movements in the market, through web site based news offerings, is remote. Web based services of this type are best considered as a way of analysing events in greater depth - perhaps before initiating a trade.

Let's take an example of this. You may believe, for instance, that the US producer price figures - due out in a few days time - will be worse than expected, and will cause a sell-off in the American market, and consequently produce a negative reaction in the FTSE 100 index, which you can profit from by buying an out-of-the-money index put option. But you need hard information to work out what the odds of this event are.

Ordinarily, this would be difficult to do. However, there are a number of web sites available that can offer help. One of the best, in my view, is the Yardeni Economic Network. This is a site operated by Dr Ed Yardeni, Deutsche Morgan Grenfell's economist in New York. The site's attraction, however, is that it offers comprehensive links to sites related to economic statistics organisation in the US and around the world.

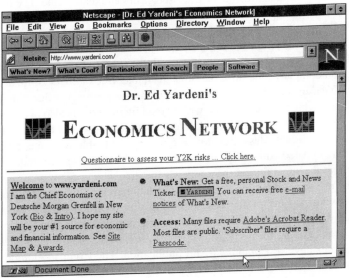

Chart 28: Yardini Economic Network.

From this, it is possible to check the historic background to the producer price numbers from an official US government site, gauge what the market is expecting, and make a judgement accordingly. The site contains a facility whereby those registering (which can include private individuals) can go on to an electronic list which will email an alert when a new commentary is added to the site. In the UK, the HM Treasury site offers the same facility for press releases emanating from this source.

Online company news and information

The observant may notice that online newspapers were not included in the preceding section. Online newspapers are obviously a useful way an investor can widen his or her reading list without inflating the paper bill to unacceptable proportions. While that includes reading about economic news, one of their best uses is as a source of company news.

The reason that some online newspapers are so good in this respect is that in the case of the *Financial Times* and the *Daily Telegraph*, their news archives are searchable. The principle is a simple one: type in the company name, if necessary restrict the search to the appropriate City and business pages to cut out any extraneous material, and any articles on the company will be displayed, complete with hyperlinks to enable them to be accessed easily and read online. The FT archive covers the last 30 days, although it is not exhaustive in its coverage of companies, while the *Telegraph's* is the largest, going back to early 1995. However, in practice for the purposes of option trading, only the most recent references are likely to be required. This system, though, does away with the need to keep a cuttings library of every option company. The information is available, free of charge online.

The *Evening Standard's* (London's evening newspaper) influential Business Day section - which is known to be widely read by traders - is also available online through the day in its five editions. A five-day archive is kept at the web site, but is not searchable. Nonetheless, this, too, represents a valuable resource, all the more so for being updated edition by edition at predictable times as different editions of the paper hit the street during the course of the day.

There are some other good resources available giving fundamental information about companies. One of the best is UK Equities Direct, part of the web site operated by the Hemmington Scott publishing group. Hemmington Scott publishes *The Company Guide*, formerly known as the *Hambro Company Guide*, as well as the Jim Slater-devised *Company REFS* publication. The Company Guide contains snapshot information on the full range of listed companies, including five-year summary accounts data, company officers, the head office contact details and the timing of announcements. UK Equities Direct, which is free, contains all this information, plus brokers consensus earnings forecasts and a share price chart, together with any additional information the company itself wishes to add.

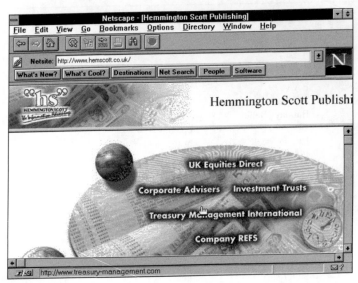

Chart 29: Equities Direct.

The REFS product is more expensive to subscribe to and contains much more detailed statistics. The REFS database is also now available on a searchable CD-Rom, which can be screened to throw up companies which fit specific financial criteria. A pay-per-view version is available at the Hemmington Scott site.

Equally useful, from the online option investor's standpoint, are corporate web sites. Very common indeed in the US, these are now spreading like wildfire to the UK corporate sector. Large companies have led the way and, at the time of writing, more than half of the FTSE 100 had corporate web sites. Though the quality of the sites is variable, many of them offer financial information. This normally takes the form of an online version of the company annual report, and access to press releases. The best of the sites (Kingfisher and Severn Trent stand out in this respect) also offer a regularly updated share price chart and email access to investor relations personnel.

Information on corporate web sites of UK stocks which have options is shown in the table. New sites are being added all the time, so it is worthwhile checking periodically with some of the sites that list them. Good sources of information on corporate sites are CAROL (Company Annual Reports On Line) and FIND (Financial Information Directory), both of which contain extensive links to corporate sites. Market Eye's web site also carries links to corporate web sites where available.

OPTION COMPANIES WITH WEB SITES

COMPANY	WEB ADDRESS (http://www...)
ASDA	asda.co.uk
BAA	baa.co.uk
BSkyB	sky.co.uk
Barclays Bank	barclays.co.uk
BP	bp.com
British Steel	britishsteel.co.uk
BT	bt.com
Cable & Wireless	cwplc.com
Centrica	centrica.co.uk
Dixons	dixons.co.uk
GEC	gec.com
GlaxoWellcome	glaxowellcome.co.uk
Grenada	grenada.co.uk
HSBC Group	hsbcgroup.com
ICI	demon.co.uk/ici/
Kingfisher	kingfisher.co.uk
LASMO	lasmo.co.uk
Marks & Spencer	marks-and-spencer.co.uk
NatWest Group	natwestgroup.com
National Power	national-power.com
Orange	orange.co.uk
P&O	p-and-o.com
Prudential	prudentialcorp.com
Railtrack	railtrack.co.uk
Reuters	reuters.com
Rolls Royce	rolls-royce.com
Royal & Sun Alliance	royal-and-sunalliance.com
Sainsbury	j-sainsbury.co.uk
Shell	shell.com
SmithKline Beecham	sb.com
Tesco	tesco.co.uk
Unilever	unilever.com
Vodafone	vodafone.com
Zeneca	zeneca.com

Finally, the availability of accounts data and press releases online is particularly important for option traders because, unlike holders of the underlying shares, they may well not receive these documents automatically. Most large companies will provide private individuals with copies of annual reports and the like, but having the information there on line is an added bonus.

Online option prices and charts

As noted in a previous chapter, for a number of years one of the best free sources of periodically updated price information was via the BBC2 CEEFAX service. In late 1996, the BBC unilaterally decided to remove this service, despite the protestations of LIFFE and many individual equity option investors. Fortunately, other alternative sources have become available, not least from LIFFE itself, which has begun posting price data on its web site, but also from other broadcasting organisations - notably BSkyB - which runs options prices on its Sky News SkyText service.

In addition, the freeing up of underlying data by the Stock Exchange has also been matched in the option area, and services such as ESI and Market Eye carry option prices on their web sites. These prices are typically in the form of a delayed continuous feed, or a system whereby prices are updated frequently, normally every 15 minutes, a considerable improvement on the old CEEFAX service which was updated around seven times daily. LIFFE's web site also contains price data and recent Reuters news for all options stocks.

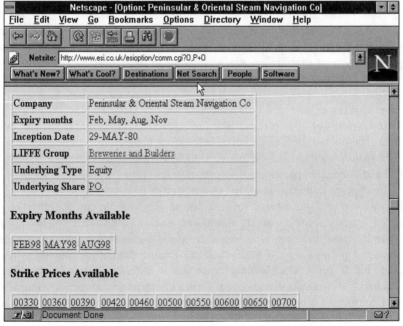

Chart 30: ESI Option Prices.

Once again, the point needs to be made that the average private investor cannot possibly compete with the professionals in terms of speed of reaction to a price change, but more frequent updating is nonetheless clearly desirable, and can be accessed free of charge or for a modest monthly fee.

We have covered the various share price charting choices, in the form of commercially available software packages, in an earlier chapter and the points made there need no reiteration. However, it is worth noting that a variety of charts are available free on the web, notably from LIFFE's own web site. LIFFE introduced these charts in the autumn of 1997. They give a snapshot of share price movements for the 70 or so option stocks available.

Private investors for the most part need look no further than this service as a source of price chart information. However, to the extent that some UK option stocks - Reuters, BAT Industries and others - are listed in New York, investors can also tap into the price charting and quote services offered by a number of web sites in the US, such as PC Quote and Quote.com, and Yahoo!. In addition DBC has a particularly good charting product at its web site.

A list of UK companies listed in the US can be found at the Moneyworld web site, where prices can also be viewed after the close of business in the UK. This should be compared with the list of UK option stocks. A variety of chart related links can be found via search directories such as Yahoo!. Yahoo!'s market summary page also has a quote facility attached, although users need to be aware of the company's stock symbol (or look it up) before using the service.

Option brokers online

Tracking broker web sites is rather like aiming at a moving target, so the comments contained below are not intended to be exhaustive, but merely to highlight the types of information available and the brokers which, at the time of writing, were offering useful and interesting packages of information for option investors.

The sites are limited in number, not specifically because UK brokers are averse to having web sites, but because many of those with sites do not offer their clients a traded options service. Among those with sites who do are Berkeley Futures (despite its name the firm also transacts option business for private investors), Durlacher, Options Direct, Charles Schwab Europe, Redmayne Bentley, Charles Stanley and Union CAL. However, each site is different, some simply offering access to basic information and option market commentary, and some going all the way up to offering a web dealing service in traded options.

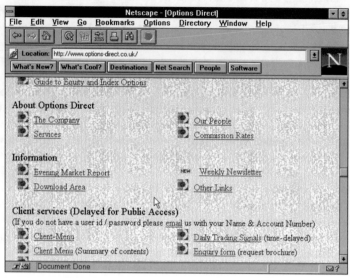

Chart 31: Options Direct Web Site.

Although those offering the latter service are currently few in number, this is an area which is changing rapidly. At the time of writing it was known that Charles Schwab Europe had definite plans to move towards offering electronic dealing in options at some point in the reasonably near future. Charles Stanley launched its Xest on-line equities dealing service via ESI in November 1997.

It is worth noting as well that electronic trading in options is big business in the US. E*Trade, the originator of web-based discount broking, reckons it accounts for around 2% of all US stock option trades, a bigger market share than it has in ordinary stock trades. The mathematical nature of option trading and evaluation makes it something that is suitable for computer analysis, as noted earlier. So what could be more natural than, after analysing an option trade on computer, to place the trade electronically as well?

Unfortunately, at the time of writing, and unlike what happens in the US, electronic trading of options is something of a misnomer. As is the case in the share market too, for the moment at least, the electronic aspect is simply the routing of the order to a dealer, and the routing of a confirmation back to the client by secure email. The UK has not yet reached the point where these trades are fully automated and 'untouched by human hand'. Consequently, the charges for electronically transmitted orders are little different from those of the normal telephone-based execution-only broker.

This may change, however, The creation of the SETS system for UK equity trading, and LIFFE's automating of its equity options trading from November 1998 opens up the possibility that US-style automated electronic trading may be possible, provided that customers' fears over the security aspects of such transactions can be allayed.

Either way, it's probably a good idea, if you happen to be selecting a broker through which to trade options, to ask whether or not they have a web site, and whether or not they plan to offer online trading of options via the web or another electronic means in the future.

Appraising brokers' web sites is fraught with difficulty, in part because different people wish to use them for different purposes. And judgements about ease of use can be clouded by the type of connection being used, speed of modem, and speed of processor of the PC being used.

Of the sites mentioned, however, those of Options Direct and Union CAL are worthy of special mention. In the case of Options Direct, the site contains much of the usual general information about the firm, but a particularly useful section accessible to the general public containing some simple spreadsheet programs related to options strategies. Client areas also contain special information including recommendations on strategies and market commentary.

Union CAL has adopted a slightly different approach, with a secure online dealing service hosted by ESI supplemented by other information, including links to sites containing downloadable software and other web links, and technical commentary (among other things) on the FTSE 100 index.

However, broker sites are changing all the time, so it is worth bookmarking the sites and checking them from time to time to see if new features have been added.

LIFFE's web presence

As mentioned earlier in this chapter LIFFE, like many other futures and options exchanges around the world, has been active on the world wide web for some time. Its site is one of the best of those operated by such exchanges, and a recent redesign has made it even more user friendly for the private investor than it was previously.

LIFFE got involved with the web, or more accurately the Internet, in 1991, when Internet access was made available to selected employees in its technology area and those in that area who needed to use email. The result was that LIFFE was able to keep up to date with developments and get its site off the ground quickly when it became obvious that the medium was likely to become more and more widely used.

Essentially, the exchange made a conscious decision to treat the site partly as an educational tool and partly as a resource for investors, rather than to use it actively to market options to web users. The site contains a variety of information in addition to those already mentioned, including information about LIFFE courses for professional and private investors alike, Exchange press releases, detailed historic data in a downloadable form for feeding into proprietary and commercial software packages, information on the technology behind the exchange, and so on.

LIFFE has redesigned the site several times in an attempt to make it more accessible to users. At the time of writing, the most recent redesign move had shifted the site away from offering information segmented by product group (stocks, bonds, short term interest rates, commodities etc) towards a clearer subdivision of the site between those areas intended for professional use, and those for private investors.

This has resulted in the creation of a 'private investor centre' at the LIFFE site, which contains all the data that such an individual investor would need, from information on courses, details of suitable software packages, equity and index option prices, downloadable data, company news and charts, and so on. This avoids the user having to spend time shifting between different parts of the wider site, with the inevitable delays caused by web traffic.

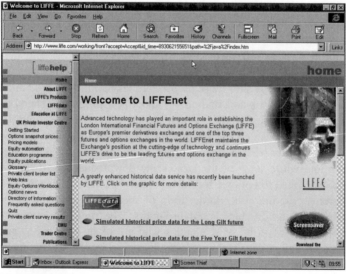

Chart 32: LIFFE Site.

The site has always been a popular one. In the first instance, many users were international, particularly from the US using the site to access end-of-day data on trading in futures contracts. Now, in parallel with increased web activity outside the US, usage of the site has grown with many private investors using the site to keep up to date on option prices. Although the situation is fluid, with web use increasing almost daily, it is clear that the site has become an established destination for option investors in the UK.

Now the figures suggest that UK users, especially private investors, may be using the site more, with the fixed group of (predominantly professional) US traders and professional advisers representing a similar level of usage, but decreasing as a proportion of the total. However, the situation is fluid.

One issue which worries many organisations setting up web sites is the degree to which they absorb management time. LIFFE's technological focus meant that it is able to operate the site with the minimum of personnel, while emails from 'surfers' have remained at a comparatively low level - an indication that the content of the site is pretty much what the average user requires.

One point is worth emphasising. This is that access to the site can involve a potential 250 or more legal jurisdictions, and LIFFE was at pains to have a carefully worded disclaimer - and make it impossible to access the site without passing through that page - to cover itself legally in respect of any potential liability arising from the use or misuse of information contained in the site. The site is considered a model in this respect, and there remain a sizeable number of other exchanges around the world where information of this type can be accessed without passing a disclaimer page.

Downloadable options software
As most keen 'surfers' are aware, the web has considerable quantities of free and low-cost resources to offer, for those prepared to take a little time to hunt them out. There are a number of ways of finding out about new programs related to options, of which probably the best are Usenet newsgroups related to this topic. The two or three best to use in this context are *misc.invest.futures*, *misc.invest.technical* and *uk.finance*, with many posts cropping up across all three.

In addition, while some of the large scale downloadable software sites have small sections related to options, for the most part specialist sites tend to be where these programs crop up, either in the form of shareware, or in the form of time-limited trial versions of commercial programs. The option community is one, however, that interests a lot of academics who are often prepared to post simple products on the web and make them available for use by the private investor.

The table below shows some examples of downloadable programs that are available either free of charge or on a shareware basis together with their web address and a brief description. Web addresses and prices sometimes change, but were correct at the time the final proofs of this chapter were returned to the publisher. A software search engine such as Download.com may well be able to locate the site if the web link stated does not appear to work. Otherwise, using a conventional search tool (such as AltaVista or Whowhere.com if the author's name is known)) to locate the source of the program may be a good substitute.

DOWNLOADABLE OPTIONS SOFTWARE

Name of program	Type	Stand-alone/ add-in	Company	Web address	Demo/ free	Price of full version
Covered Option Writer	Strategy	SA	The Underground Software Grp	http://www.tugsg.com	Demo	$40
Option Oracle	Pricing/strategy	SA	Deltasoft Financial Technologies	http://www.option-oracle.com	Demo	$695
Option Pro	Pricing/strategy	SA	Essex Trading Co	http://www.essextrading.com	Demo	$795
Option Simulator	Pricing/strategy	SA	Bay Options	http://www.bayoptions.com	Demo	$795
Option Wizard	Pricing/strategy	AI	John Sarkett	http://option-wizard.com	Demo	$99
OptionCalc	Pricing/strategy	SA	Austin Software	http://www.austin-soft.com	Demo	$295
OptionLab	Pricing/strategy	SA	Mantic Software	http://www.manticsoft.com	Demo	$90
OptionVue	Pricing/strategy	SA	OptionVue	http://www.optionvue.com	Demo	$1695
!Options	Pricing/strategy	AI(Fnctns)	Ray Steele	http://pilot.msu.edu/user/steelera/!options	Free	n/a
Optimum	Pricing/strategy	SA	Nigel Webb Software	http://www.warp9.org/nwsoft/index.html	Free	n/a
Option Driver	Pricing/strategy	AI	FIS Ltd	http://www.download.com/opdrv32.zip	Free	$49.50
SmartLog	Trading log	AI	IME Corporation	http://ourworld.compuserve.com/homepages/svirsky/smartlog.htm	Free	$39.95

The variety of programs available indicates the interest that options stir up, especially in the US. However, when downloading a program (just as when buying one) it is worth checking thoroughly the ability of the package being downloaded to work with UK data. For most packages this issue may not arise, since they will simply calculate option prices, the 'greeks' and other variables, based on the data fed into them. In some cases, however, the need to calculate historic volatility may demand a price series for the underlying to be input.

Often, however, the demand will simply be for a string of data to be available in simple text (CSV) format, and it is comparatively easy to download the price series for an underlying in this form from a free price source. Web sites like Market Eye's, for example, offer this facility. The compatibility issue is worth checking (possibly by emailing the web site concerned before beginning the download process).

There are many other sites available offering access to a range of software packages. The best is probably Wall Street Directory, which has a comprehensive range of products for investors, including option price software. LIFFE also produces a booklet summarising the various types of option and technical analysis software available, and the features they offer. Other sites worth checking out for links to, and reviews of software products include Investorama, INO, NumaWeb and Wall Street Street Software.

At the time of writing, the free software products that I have found most useful include a spreadsheet add-in called !Options available from Ray Steele's web site at Michigan State University. This supplements basic Excel functions and so can be used to value options contained elsewhere in, say, the spreadsheet an investor might use to monitor his or her investments.

The Options Direct web site contains a spreadsheet that can calculate the returns available from a covered write strategy (see chapter 6 for recap on this strategy).

A product called Covered Option Writer is available from The Underground Software group site. This enables series of covered write strategies to be ranked on the basis of various variables, such as their 'static' or 'if called ' returns.

Investors should, however, check out all these products thoroughly for themselves before using them. Any preferences expressed here are purely personal and should not be taken as, or implied to be a recommendation.

Other options sites
The web has a vast reserve of sites related to options and to the wider derivatives scene. These include, in particular, derivatives exchanges, firms offering professional risk management and option valuation software, as well as specialist publications and newsletters devoted to the topic. How much one reads is really a function of how deeply one wishes to go into the subject, although it

is perhaps worth noting when focusing on the UK options markets, and the companies within it, that many 'educational' sites have a US flavour.

Several exchanges in the US and Europe offer web sites. Good exchange sites include the Chicago Board Options Exchange, Philadelphia Exchange, Deutsche Borse, and OM Group - all of which have extensive material on options.

The best sites include easy graphics, near real-time prices, searchability, fast access to historical data, and links to related sites.

Among specialist publications, *Futures and Options World*, a well known publication read by professional and amateur traders alike, has a web site. Its counterpart, perhaps, can be found in the web site of Applied Derivatives Trading, which is a wholly online newsletter devoted to derivatives (including options). A similar publication, of a more theoretical bent, is the *Electronic Journal of Financial Risk* (or NetExposure).

Sites devoted to specific option strategies crop up occasionally and one, with a US bias, is Allinthemoney, devoted to information about covered call writing. Its US bias is a disadvantage, however, as is the $49 per month subscription, which puts it out of reach of all but the most ardent enthusiast.

A more general site is Traders Haven. Although originating in the US, this site contains stockmarket-related links that can be sorted by country, by topic or alphabetically. The links include other search tools, supranational organisations, and other information providers.

Mentioning these sites does not imply an endorsement: they are simply a random selection designed to give an idea of the variety of resources available.

Yahoo!'s investment section has a comprehensive range of links to futures and options related web sites, and is a useful starting point. Of particular note is a link in the 'glossaries' section to Derivatives Research Unincorporated, which contains a series of more than 60 essays on various aspects of the derivatives scene, including many relevant to traders. All of the essays are written in non-technical language. Equally important, the site contains a 'list of lists', giving links to large scale compendiums of information on options, including some of those mentioned above.

Summary

1. The world wide web has huge resources which can be of use to would-be option traders.

2. Economic data is available from many different sources on the web, including governmental statistical organisations, and investment banks. Much of the information is available free of charge. Online feeds from news organisations are also available.

3. Company information is particularly good on the web. Sources include publishers of reference works who (to date) offer free online access, and the increasing number of corporate web sites, as well as the searchable archives of online broadsheet newspapers.

4. Options prices, typically delayed by around 15 minutes, are now available free of charges from a number of sources, including LIFFE's own web site. Similarly LIFFE's web site contains price charts and five days of Reuters news for each equity option's underlying security.

5. LIFFE's web site has recently been redesigned to make it more 'user-friendly' for the private investor. Information relevant to private investors trading options is gathered together in a 'private investor centre'.

6. Some brokers offering a traded option dealing service have web sites. However, in many cases these have little interactive content. The exceptions are Options Direct, which has downloadable options software, and Union CAL, offering a secure online option order routing service.

7. Free options software can be downloaded from a number of sources on the web, and there is a range of sites offering commercially available packages. Data compatibility should be checked, but the universality of the mathematics behind options means that many packages work equally well wherever they are used.

8. A vast range of other sites is available on the web, some dealing with futures as well as options. These range from futures and options exchanges, through publications such as newsletters, to brokers, to lists of links to any number of vaguely related sites. Care needs to be taken when accessing these sites.

9. Investors are strongly advised to concentrate on those sites related to options. It is very important, too, to master trading in UK equity and index options before progressing to other markets. Stick to the market you know.

APPENDIX

GLOSSARY OF WEB ADDRESSES

NAME	WEB ADDRESS
News	
Applied Derivatives Trading	http://www.adtrading.com
Bloomberg Personal	http://www.bloomberg.com
CNNfn	http://www.cnnfn.com
DejaNews	http://www.dejanews.com
Electronic Telegraph	http://www.telegraph.co.uk
European Business News	http://www.ebn.co.uk
Financial Times	http://www.ft.com
(London) *Evening Standard*	http://www.standard.co.uk
Newslink	http://www.newslink.org
Reuters	http://www.reuters.com
The Press Association	http://www.pa.press.net
Times/Sunday Times	http://www.the-times.co.uk
Wall Street Journal	http://www.wsj.com
Jumping Off Points	
Business Information on the Internet	http://www.dis.strath.ac.uk/business/
Finance OnLine	http://www.finance-online.com
Financial Information Network	http://www.finetwork.com
FIND	http://www.find.co.uk
Global OnLine Directory	http://www.god.co.uk
Global Trader	http://www.bluewave.co.uk/globaltrader
Hot Links for Traders	http://www.io.com/%7Egibbonsb/wahoo.html
Internect	http://www.inect.co.uk
Investorama	http://www.investorama.com
Lenape Investment Corporation	http://www.enter.net/~rsauers/

NAME	WEB ADDRESS
Mauro Magnani's Finance Area	http://www.tsi.it/contrib/audies/finarea.html
Moneyweb	http://www.moneyweb.co.uk
Moneyworld	http://www.moneyworld.co.uk
NumaWeb	http://www.numa.com
Qualisteam	http://www.qualisteam.com
Trader's Financial Resource Guide	http://www.libertynet.org/~beausang
UK Index	http://www.ukindex.co.uk
UK Web Directory	http://www.ukdirectory.com
Waldemars List	http://apollo.netservers.com/ ~waldemar/list.shtm

Brokers on the Web

Charles Stanley	http://www.xest.com
Durlacher	http://www.durlacher.com
E*Trade	http://www.etrade.com
Electronic Share Information (ESI)	http://www.esi.co.uk
Infotrade	http://www.infotrade.co.uk
Options Direct	http://www.options-direct.co.uk
Schwab	http://www.schwab.co.uk

Prices and Data

Company Annual Reports Online	http://www.carol.co.uk
Corporate Reports	http://www.corpreports.co.uk
Datastream/ICV	http://www.market-eye.co.uk
DBC	http://www.dbceuro.com
FT Information	http://www.info.ft.com/companies/
PC Quote Europe	http://www.pcquote-europe.co.uk
PC Quote	http://www.pcquote.com
Prestel	http://www.citiservice.co.uk
Quote.com	http://www.quote.com
UK Equities Direct	http://www.hemscott.com
Yardeni Economic Network	http://www.yardeni.com

Software

Download.com	http://www.download.com
Shareware.com	http://www.shareware.com

NAME	WEB ADDRESS
University of California at San Marcos	http://coyote.csusm.edu/winworld/diverse.html
Wall Street Directory	http://www.wsdinc.com
Wall Street Software	http://www.fastlane.net/homepages/wallst/wallst.html
Winsite	http://www.winsite.com

Governments and Regulators

Bank of England	http://www.bankofengland.co.uk
CCTA	http://www.open.gov.uk
Central Office for Information	http://www.coi.gov.uk
UK Treasury	http://www.hm-treasury.gov.uk
US Treasury	http://www.ustreas.gov

Exchanges

Chicago Board of Trade	http://www.cbot.com
Chicago Board Options Exchange	http://www.cboe.com
Chicago Mercantile Exchange	http://www.cme.com
Deutsche Borse	http://www.exchange.de
LIFFE	http://www.liffe.com
MATIF (Paris)	http://www.matif.fr
New York Mercantile	http://www.nymex.com
OM Stockholm	http://www.omgroup.com
Philadelphia Stock Exchange	http://www.phlx.com
SAFEX (South Africa)	http://www.safex.co.za
SIMEX	http://www.simex.com.sg
Sydney Derivatives Exchange	http://www.sfe.com.au

PRIVATE CLIENT COURSES IN EQUITY AND INDEX OPTIONS

As part of their continuing commitment to the development of private client option business in the UK, the (equity products) retail marketing team of LIFFE hold regular private client courses throughout the UK.

Introductory Seminars
Evening seminars designed to introduce equity and index options to new users wishing to incorporate these derivative products into their investment portfolios. The seminar provides an insight into the myths and benefits of using equity and index products and gives you the opportunity to find out how they can be used to enhance your investments. The seminars are aimed at private clients with little or no knowledge of options. The seminars are presented by LIFFE staff and further information is supplemented by numerous publications made available for further reading.

Intermediate Workshops
Afternoon workshops designed for private clients who would like to gain further information about the use of options as investment tools. Topics covered will include options profit and loss profiles, basic strategies, covered call writing and portfolio enhancement. The workshops will be presented by LIFFE staff. Further information is supplemented by numerous publications, including a copy of the Equity Options Workbook.

The London seminars are held at LIFFE, Cannon Bridge, London and the regional events are held at suitable hotels.

EQUITY OPTIONS WORKBOOK

LIFFE has published a self–teach type workbook which is now available. It is a comprehensive study manual for private investors and brokers who have little or no knowledge of options. The workbook explains the workings of the market place, the contracts traded, the users and the uses of options. The aim of the workbook being to provide "hands–on" experience of the subject with practical exercises throughout and with the answers at the back.

In brief, the contents are:

Introduction
An introduction to the exchange and its equity options. Who uses the market, how and why they use the contracts.

The Products
What is an option, basic terminology and contract specifications. The effect of corporate events. Index options.

Simple Strategies
The benefits of options. Typical investment decisions using options. Choices for holders and writers. Buying and selling calls and puts.

Further Strategies
More sophisticated uses combining the basic four option positions.

Pricing
Components of an option price: intrinsic and time values. Factors affecting an option price. Premium movement trends. The Greeks. Price dissemination.

Practicalities
How to find a broker and the services available. The contract note. What to do before trading.

The Market Place

LIFFE's role, its trading hours, methods and participants. Dealing procedures and the Public Limit Order Board Settlement.

Clearing

The London Clearing House and its functions. The clearing structure, margin and collateral. Exercise and allocation. Delivery and settlement.

For an application form and/or further information about the private client courses held by LIFFE or about the Equity Options Workbook, please contact Kirsty Grant on 0171–379 2486.

INDEX

Page references followed by an asterisk, as in 88*,
are to explanations of terms

A

B

backspread	132*, 144
banks	23
bear call spread	134-137
bear spread	132*
Big Bang 1986	20, 45
binomial valuing method	120
Black-Scholes valuing method	19, 120
book structure	13
broker	*see* stockbroker
building societies	23
bull call spread	131-134
bull spread	132*
business environment	62
butterfly spread	132*, 140-143
buy-write strategy	88*, 93-96

C

calculation of index option value at expiry	104
calendar spread	132*, 137-139
call option	10, 16*, 17, 28 *and see* option and options
CAROL (Company Annual Reports On Line)	167
cash outcome of index option	103

D

E

F

G

H

I

J

L

M

option and options

P

R

S

T

traditional options	18, 25
tranquil share	65
"trend is your friend, the"	148
trends	148-151
tulip bulb boom and bust	19
turning points	62, 155

U

UK Equities Direct	166
uncovered writing	88* *and see* naked writing
Union CAL	172
United States of America	21, 45, 103, 171
upward price target	60

V

variation margin	88
vega	121*
vertical spread	132*, 137
volatility	15, 25*, 34-36, 65, 116, 120*, 151
historic	65
implied	65
importance	122-123

W

walking-up the position	95
Wall Street crash 1929	19
warnings	
complex trades	145
naked writing	87, 88*, 99
options characteristics	23
web sites	*see* online information
Welles-Wilder relative strength index (RSI)	157-158
writer	29-30

Y

Yahoo!	170, 177
Yardeni Economic Network	165-166

Z

Zulu Principle, The	61